LASTING MARRIAGES

Men and Women Growing Together

Richard A. Mackey
and
Bernard A. O'Brien

PRAEGER

Westport, Connecticut
London

Library of Congress Cataloging-in-Publication Data

Mackey, Richard A.
    Lasting marriages : men and women growing together / Richard A.
Mackey and Bernard A. O'Brien.
        p. cm.
    Includes bibliographical references (p.   ) and index.
    ISBN 0–275–95075–1 (hardcover : acid-free paper). — ISBN
0–275–95076–X (pbk. : acid-free paper)
    1. Marriage—United States. 2. Marriage—United States—Case
studies. 3. Married people—United States. 4. Married people—
United States—Case studies. I. O'Brien, Bernard A. II. Title.
HQ536.M24   1995
306.81′0973—dc20   95–3336

British Library Cataloguing in Publication Data is available.

Library of Congress Catalog Card Number: 95–3336
ISBN: 0–275–95075–1 (hc)
ISBN: 0–275–95076–X (pbk)

First published in 1995

Praeger Publishers, 88 Post Road West, Westport, CT 06881
An imprint of Greenwood Publishing Group, Inc.

Printed in the United States of America

The paper used in this book complies with the
Permanent Paper Standard issued by the National
Information Standards Organization (Z39.48–1984).

10 9 8 7 6 5 4 3 2 1

To the memory of
LYNN and LEIF
whose life together had just begun

Contents

Acknowledgments

We want to thank several individuals who helped us in carrying out this research and in preparing this book. We are indebted to the following Counseling Psychology doctoral students at Boston College who conducted the interviews: Christine Demment, Christine Hamel, Laura Kanter, Susan Mengden, and Jana Podbelski. Other students who made significant contributions to our work included Tiffany Cannon, Beth Gouse, Stephen Rossetti, and Shawn Sullivan. Although too numerous to acknowledge by name, we appreciate the assistance of other students in the School of Education, the Graduate School of Arts and Sciences, and the Graduate School of Social Work who participated in one form or another in this project.

The administration at Boston College was very supportive of our work, especially in providing us with grants to cover research expenses. In particular, we wish to thank Deans June Gary Hopps, Diana C. Pullin, and Donald J. White. Several colleagues were very helpful with the research procedures and in reviewing drafts of the manuscript. They included Sandra Crump, Donna Ferullo, Scott Kinder, and James Mahalik.

We are indebted to the secretarial staff who prepared drafts of the text. To Mary Kelley and Dorothy Artesani Cochrane we express our thanks; to

Marguerite Tierney we acknowledge a special thank you for her care in preparing the final copy of the manuscript.

To our spouses, Eileen Mackey and Evelyn O'Brien, we are grateful for their support throughout this project. Each of them also made extraordinary contributions to editing the manuscript.

Finally, we thank the people who so generously gave of themselves to participate as respondents in this study. Their openness and eloquence about their lives are evident throughout this book.

Prologue

The expression, *Growing Together*, in the subtitle of this book was taken from an interview with a 57-year-old man who was trying to convey what his marriage of twenty-five years meant to him: "There is a growing together . . . like a tree around a boulder underneath the ground. The root eventually goes around it."

The metaphor of the roots of a tree growing around a boulder reflected the depth, diversity, and dynamism of experiences which 120 spouses from sixty marriages shared with us. This book tells their stories—the stories of joy, suffering, conflict, doubt, and reconciliation—as they lived out their lives together from the first time they met, through the rearing of their children and into the empty-nest years. They rarely moved boulders, yet they found ways of adapting to each other, which left them more rather than less satisfied with their long-lasting relationships.

Marriage has undergone many changes over the last few decades, not the least of which is that couples who stay together will remain together for longer periods of time in view of increased life expectancies. As longevity extends into the seventies, eighties, and beyond, it is critical to identify the significant dynamics that contribute to satisfaction among couples in stable marriages. The research on which this book is based explored stable marriages from the perspectives of husbands and wives as each talked about the meaning of their relationships from initial attraction to the present time. Focusing on the experiences of spouses throughout their marriages, the book responds to a recognized need for research on understanding lasting marital relationships.

Historically, the nature of the marital relationship has been assessed through an examination of two dimensions: marital stability and quality. Marital stability refers to whether or not a marriage is still together. Understanding the quality of a marriage requires a subjective evaluation of the marital relationship. A changing and multidimensional concept, quality is discussed in the literature under a variety of headings such as marital satisfaction, marital happiness, or adjustment. Although some researchers suggest that marital stability and quality are related, the evidence for such a relationship is not clear. Studies show that some marriages of high quality end in divorce, whereas others of low quality remain intact. Our research explored the factors that contributed to long-lasting marriages.

Based on in-depth interviews with husbands and wives conducted from 1990 to 1994 by skilled clinicians, the book explores how spouses adapted to each other from the early years of marriage, through the parenting years, and into the post-parenting or empty-nest years. All couples had been married at least twenty years; most had been married over thirty years. None were in therapy for marital conflicts, although practically all experienced the kinds of problems typical of most married couples. Purposively selected for inclusion in the research were groups that represented religious, ethnic, racial, and educational diversity. Focal questions elicited observations from individual spouses about the dimensions of their lives together. The richness of this approach was enhanced by using both quantitative and qualitative methods of data analysis.

Although the organization of the book is shaped by statistical findings, its presentation is human centered. We identify themes that emerged from the data, and then we use excerpts from transcripts of interviews to illustrate those themes. The discussion moves back and forth between conceptualization of themes and illustrations of them with quotes from individual spouses. We have allowed these people to speak for themselves because they so eloquently conveyed the meaning of their relationships over the years. The primary focus is on gender, or how men and women are similar and how they are different, which is deepened by examining social class differences: blue- and-white collar couples; religious differences: Jewish, Protestant, and Catholic couples; racial and ethnic differences: white,

African-American, and Mexican-American couples. The sample represents diversity not found in previous research on marriage.

Each chapter focuses on an important theme in these marital relationships which were elicited during the interviews. The organization of the book follows the sequence of topics explored in the interviews. In the first chapter, we discuss the beginnings of the relationships and the recollections of how respondents were initially attracted to their future spouses. Chapters 2 to 7 focus on dimensions of marriage as they evolved over time. Collective themes emerging from the interviews are explored in relationship to gender, ethnicity, religion, and education. The second chapter discusses the roles of spouses and how couples experienced interpersonal fit in their relationships. Relational values of trust, respect, understanding, and sensitivity are explored, as is the quality of communication throughout the three phases of marriage. Chapter 3 presents the nature of conflict within these marriages and how spouses handled interpersonal differences. The fourth chapter addresses sex and sexuality, which includes the sexual relationship, its importance, and the ways that both physical and psychological intimacy are expressed. Decision making is discussed in the following chapter, where the observations of respondents about their individual decision-making styles are explored. Also, the joint decision-making styles of couples which are conceptualized along a continuum from mutuality to separateness are examined. The parenting dimension of marriage is the subject of Chapter 6: it focuses on how couples adapted to the realities of caring for children during infancy, latency, and adolescence and the effect of child-rearing on marital relationships. In the final chapter, the illusive concept of marital satisfaction is discussed. Culled from the data are several themes that contributed to marital satisfaction as these people live out their lives together in middle and old age.

The book builds on the existing literature related to marriage; its presentation is unique. First, the subjects of the study represent ethnic diversity. Nearly half of the respondents in the research on which this book is based were Mexican Americans and African Americans. Second, over half of the sample was employed in blue-collar occupations. Third, Catholics, Protestants, and Jews were included in the research since religious affiliation was assumed to have a relationship to marital quality. (See Appendix A for details about the characteristics of respondents.) Fourth, the book presents the experiences of husbands and wives as they were reported by these individuals. Although scientific procedures were employed to code, organize, and analyze the data (see Appendixes B, C, and D for more details about the research methodology), the presentation relies on the observations of respondents as reported in their own words. Themes are discussed and previous literature is integrated into the text, but the eloquence and poignancy of individual respondents are not compromised by professional jargon. Fifth, none of the spouses had any substantial psychotherapy for marital problems. Thus, the discussion of their skills in adapting to marriage over time represents strengths not attributable to professional intervention, a feature with which most readers can identify. Sixth, to explore success at marriage through the eyes of older couples who are a growing population is a unique feature of this book.

In reviewing the transcripts of the interviews and field notes, we were impressed with the openness and honesty of respondents to our questions. We appreciated their generosity in sharing rich and intimate details of their long-lasting marriages. To respect their privacy, all identifying information about them has been disguised, which includes the use of fictitious names throughout the book.

—1—

Looking Back: Initial Attraction

. . . it was an instant recognition of a kindred soul . . .

This book begins where people in these long-lasting marriages began: in their memories of what attributes drew them to an individual with whom they were to spend a lifetime. Recollections of initial attraction included those extrinsic qualities that may have been evident when people first met as well as intrinsic qualities that emerged as individuals came to know one another.

Burgess, Wallin and Schultz (1954) observed forty years ago that there may never be a clear explanation of the reason(s) why one person falls in love with someone rather than anyone. After reviewing the research on initial attraction vis-à-vis our data, we are sympathetic with that observation. To a considerable extent, the expression, "falling in love," remains a mystery despite numerous studies on the topic. Our findings resonate with various hypotheses that have been derived from those studies and offer a few more clues to understanding what attracts one person to another, the initial step along the path to a loving relationship, and a seasoned marriage.

Because the data suggested that initial attraction was a complex phenomenon, a view of the findings as a whole is presented through a biopsychosocial lens that explores five patterns of initial attraction:

- Spontaneous attraction
- Ambivalent attraction
- Sexual attraction as a prelude to psychosocial connection
- Symmetrical attraction fueled by similarities
- Complementary attraction powered by differences

AN OVERVIEW

Previous research along with the data from our study suggested that
several interacting dynamics stimulated initial attraction. A perspective that
included biological, psychological, and social dynamics made more sense
than thinking about initial attraction along one dimension. In adopting a
holistic perspective, we assumed that no single theory or independent
variable offered a good enough explanation for understanding attractions
that gave birth to the process of falling in love. We understood initial
attraction as a phenomenon resulting from the interaction of physical,
psychological, and social dynamics played out in highly unique but not
equally powerful ways for each couple. For some, sexual attraction was a
primary force but rarely in isolation from other intrinsic qualities that
emerged as time passed. These intrinsic qualities included personal attributes such as a sense of humor and kindness. Other people also identified
cultural commonalities with their potential spouse such as ethnicity and
religion.

Not surprisingly, the recollections of 78 percent of the individuals were
positive in nature. Eighteen percent of the respondents recalled initial
feelings of ambivalence about their future spouses. Three times as many
women as men reported ambivalent reactions [$X^2 (2, N = 120) = 10.63, p =
.005$]. In addition to differences by gender, the data also revealed differences
by ethnicity. More African-American women than others remembered
feeling ambivalent in their initial meetings with their partners [$X^2 (2, N =
120) = 9.92, p = .04$]. Four women said they had negative reactions in their
first encounters with their future spouses.

Even when the childhood relationships of individuals were conflictual,
their attraction to one another at a later time was positive. Edward, a
44-year-old truck driver, remembered the attraction to his wife of twenty-
three years. He had recently returned from three years of military duty and

had been told by his mother to find another place to live. In contrast to his wife's highly cohesive family, Edward's family was fragmented and quite chaotic. Edward speaks of his first encounter with Eve after not seeing her for eight years when she had moved with her family to the suburbs:

> Her looks. It's funny, me and Eve we grew up together. I knew Eve since she was 7 and hated her guts all through Junior High. I used to call her fatso and stuff like that when I saw her on the street. I was nursing a hangover one Sunday and her friend came over and says let's take a ride and hang out. . . . I didn't want to go but I just grabbed a paper and we went. Never looked where we were going. Where were we going? Down . . . to see Eve. I says: "Porkie?" He says: "Yeah!" I go, "Great," cause we used to fight all the time. We get there and this girl comes out . . . I remember she had this younger sister . . . , and I says, "Hello . . . ," oh! it's Eve! Her eyeballs clicked . . . it just went from there. I called as soon as I could . . . and we went out. Eve was this very special person. I didn't know it at the time. I've learned that through our years of marriage. But she's special and she just won a spot in my heart.

His 43-year-old spouse describes the paradox of being attracted to Edward after their childhood relationship which was not positive at all:

> I don't know because all those years I hated him. I don't know. Oh, my heart just went yeah! It was there.

The puzzling nature of attraction was illustrated in the stories of these two people. Although they were from similar socioeconomic backgrounds, the internal functioning of each family was very different. So upset were Eve's parents with the return of the neighborhood menace, as Edward was known, that they actively tried to discourage Eve from marrying him. The initial sexual attraction was implicit yet obvious in their memories. The road to building an alliance between them was strewn with serious obstacles. Perhaps, more than any other couple in our study, their marriage showed the interplay of individual developmental dynamics with those in the marriage itself. Eve appeared to be an object of constancy in a relationship that was often under severe strain. Yet, they survived and in middle age were experiencing a rapprochement in their love for one another which, perhaps, was present on that Sunday afternoon.

The beginnings of other relationships were not encumbered by as much conflict. Melinda, a 60-year-old professional woman of African-American decent, recalled her attraction to Mark, her husband of thirty-two years:

> Let me start with the easy thing first. Physically, I think it was his smile. But beyond that, he just has an approach of creating a feeling of comfort and a genuine interest in the person to whom he's speaking, and the kinds of qualities that would make anybody a much liked person. And that's the kind of person that he is. And beyond that, it's all the insights and the intellect that you learn about later. But initially, it was a meeting in church, those are the things that really attracted me.

Melinda spoke eloquently to the need for understanding the dynamics of attraction in terms of time and in relation to several interrelated variables. When women talked of their initial attraction as physical, it was usually in relation to a pleasing characteristic. For Melinda, that was her future husband's smile. Beyond that spark which ignited the loving relationship between them, psychosocial qualities became increasingly important. Symmetry in race, religion, and education provided a supportive matrix within which the relationship developed.

Temporal factors, to which Melinda and Edward spoke, need to be integrated into a model for understanding how initial attraction may have changed as time passed. Some individuals shifted from not being attracted to the other person to being attracted as they got to know that person. Others, for whom the initial attraction was exclusively or primarily sexual, became attracted to psychological qualities as they came to know the other person. The latter was true for Mark, Melinda's husband of the same age, race, and educational background:

> I went to church and I was sitting there, and I saw her in the choir, and I was impressed with her physical attractiveness. And also she had long hair in those years. And I got to know her basically through some other people that I was staying with. My landlady had said: "I suggest you meet her," which I did. And the rest is history.

Melinda commented on the evolution of their relationship from one that was motivated initially by mutual sexual attraction to one that was nurtured and sustained by several psychosocial attributes not fully understood even today:

> I think it probably took him a little longer to see things in me that are comparable to those internal things that I saw in him, because I'm not that open and that easily accessible. . . . I think it probably was a sense of family, my own family. He liked the fact that I was very devoted to church work. And as far as personality is concerned, I'm not sure that I can clearly say what it was . . .

Among some couples, especially those from Mexican-American backgrounds, social dynamics, which included families connected to each other within a cohesive cultural milieu, were central to understanding initial attraction. Surprisingly, that theme was not common among African-American couples in view of the strong value that ethnic group places on collateral relationships within the family of origin (Pinderhughes, 1989). The apparent glitch in the data was related to the high rate of cutoff from families of origin among African Americans, 71 percent of whom had moved to the Northeast from other parts of the country. In contrast to other couples, almost half of Mexican-American couples had known one another since childhood. For example, Beto, a 58-year-old skilled tradesman married for thirty-seven years to Buena, told us of the history of their relationship:

> I knew her all my life. She lived one block from where I lived . . . we were friends growing up . . . my parents were her parents' godfather and godmother. After I got in the service we started writing to each other . . . I thought that she was the one that I was going to marry, and when I came back, we just got closer . . . I knew her all of my life, and we had been pretty close. I used to pull her pigtails you know, when we were little.

Buena remembered:

> I was 3 years old when I first met my husband. We lived across the street from each other. We used to play together. . . . All our lives. We used to walk to school together . . . you know how that goes, we would sit next to each other, we'd line up together to go eat, in school . . . so we were always together.

Within certain cultures, social dynamics may be more influential than other factors in shaping the attraction of one person for another. Even within a fairly homogeneous group, such as working-class Mexican Americans, however, that was true for most individuals but not for all. Beta and Buena had less choice than Mark and Melinda or Edward and Eve about whom each would marry. Partly, that was because of economic poverty. Beta and Buena simply did not have as many opportunities to meet other people outside of their immediate neighborhood. The concept of "family" appeared more important than other values related to the marital relationship alone. Mexican Americans talked of marriage within the context of family, which was very different from other couples.

The stories of these six people reflected the diversity and complexity of inner and outer dynamics involved in romantic attractions. Even though themes emerged from the data in relation to gender and culture, what attracted individuals to one another was as varied as the people themselves.

SPONTANEOUS ATTRACTION

Spontaneous attraction involved the instantaneous and unambivalent conviction that one was going to marry the other person. Seventy-eight percent of the individuals were attracted to their future spouse when they first met but did not experience the kind of visceral reaction of Alicia, a Mexican-American woman who, at the age of 18, remembered:

> When he walked in, he had on some khaki pants and . . . if you've ever seen the Beverly Hillbillies . . . those boots that granny wears. That's the kind of shoes that he had on and just a plain old green shirt. I don't remember. It was a light shirt and I looked at him and I told this friend of mine that that's the guy I'm going to marry and she said I was crazy, that I didn't even know him. I said that I was going to get to know him and I'm going to marry him. So I started trying to figure out what his name was and for the longest time I called him Ben because that's what I thought his name was, and he was real quiet and he kept answering to Ben until one day I was telling our boss, and she was saying, I know that you and Armando are getting real close . . . you're too young and he's older. I said, "Who's Armando," and she said, "Armando, the guy that you like," and I said his name was Armando? I thought his name was Ben, and it was real funny because he would never correct me. And I fell in love with him the day I met him, and through the years it has just grown deeper and deeper and people say there is no such thing as love at first sight, but to me it was and it was real. . . . That might have been one of the reasons why I was attracted to him—he told me he had a mother and father, and sisters and brothers—the family unit that I never had—and that might have had something to do with it.

To the same question, Armando recalled that Alicia was twelve years younger, and he was attracted by her personality and her unusual hair style. Because of the differences in their ages, he remembered moving slowly into the relationship—quite a contrast to the memories of his wife of thirty-seven years.

We wonder what generated spontaneous attraction. Perhaps, in this case, Alicia offered a clue when she said that she was attracted not only to Armando, but also to the family of which she felt deprived, which fits with our earlier observation about the importance of family to Mexican-American couples. Although sexuality was probably an implicit dynamic in the spontaneity of Alicia to Armando, it was identified explicitly by Freeman, a 70-year-old Jewish male married over forty-four years:

> I had a date with a girlfriend of hers, and she happened to be at the same party that we were at . . . for some reason, I just saw her and that was it. That was the end of my date with the other girl. Very strong sexual attraction. That much I can tell you. Uh, I don't know, I just liked her smile and the way she acted, she felt good in my arms when we used to go dancing, went dancing that first night, in fact; I can't really tell you . . . I want to tell you something strange: the first time I met her, I went back and told an aunt of mine, I've met the girl I'm gonna marry.

The "chemistry" between Alicia and Armando may have explained the strong sexual valency in their relationship from its beginnings. Given the length of time since all of these couples had initially met, instantaneous sexual attraction along with the conviction that this was "the one" may have played an important role in other relationships. Sexual mores of the era certainly did not support spontaneous sexual attraction as a basis for marriage. We wonder, too, how much the sexual standards of that time, compared to today, may have reinforced suppression of memories.

Some research has suggested that nonverbal cues play an important role in strengthening sexual attraction between males and females (Moore & Butler, 1989). Individuals may not be fully aware of these subtle cues that may serve as precursors to further sexual involvement. Givens (1978) believed that sexual relationships may be negotiated, in part, through a universal set of behavioral signs. We can only wonder about the reciprocal nature of spontaneous attractions, but we assume that the response of the future spouse was critical to the development of relationships that led to marriage. Reciprocity, after all, is the vehicle of nurturing love.

AMBIVALENT ATTRACTION

Think of initial attraction along a continuum with a positive pole at one end and a negative one at the other end. Ambivalence lies along the continuum. Some level of ambivalence is natural to human relationships. Twenty-two percent of people in this study, mostly women, recalled their initial attraction with some ambivalence. Rarely was the memory of a purely negative nature. Of the four people who recalled feeling repelled by the man who would eventually become their husbands, three were African Americans. Carol recalled her first reaction to Carl:

I wasn't attracted to him. I thought he was arrogant and very forward the
first time I met him.

It was enlightening to hear this 51-year-old woman reflect on the development of her relationship. Carl was seven years older than Carol and had
a "reputation." She saw only what he could allow the world to see: the
arrogant, outspoken, aggressive pursuer. Only later would he tell her of his
inner thoughts and feelings that had been obscured by a tough outer shell.
From that point on, according to her, the relationship began to change and
continued to change throughout their thirty-three-year marriage.

For some people, ambivalence was mutual and fed by personal characteristics which they had in common. Homero and Herminia, a Mexican-
American couple married for twenty-nine years, illustrated ambivalent
attraction based on similarities:

HOMERO: I don't know. We were in the Student Council of the high school
together. It was real interesting because she was very strong-willed and I was
too. We were both officers and we argued. She fought her point and I fought
mine. I kind of respected her for that. Other than that, it was just getting to
know her. We went to a few functions through the school with the Student
Council; as officers we went together, and we just started dating what little
we could because her parents were very strict ... I just figured, you know,
being like my dad, you have your values. I looked at her, I looked at her
background, her family and knew that this would be the woman to raise a
family with.

HERMINIA: We were both in the Student Council and it wasn't so much
attraction, well, I guess it was attraction, but the impression of him was, golly,
I just can't stand that guy. He was so pushy and always wanted to have the
upper hand and we would argue the point on the floor, so this was like
freshman year, sophomore year, and we were like acquaintances, friends, and
he had an office in his club ... Through the Student Council is where we did
most of our work together ... we had to attend, what they called, conferences
at other schools together; so it was at that time, it wasn't so much when we
were in a large group at school, it was when we were in a smaller groups,
going to one of the conferences or something, that we were friendlier. I didn't
have a car, so I rode with him and his friends. I finally started talking one on
one and noticing what he had to say, and I noticed that he was a very caring
and sensitive person, and I'd say that it was our junior and senior year when
it clicked.

Like Carl and Carol, Herminia began to see a different side of Homero as the relationship unfolded. Unlike Carl and Carol, their ambivalence was based on personal qualities that were symmetrical. Their strengths as leaders in the student community led them to compete with each other. No doubt, the conflict must have been exacerbated by cultural norms that structured different roles for males and females. Homero probably experienced significant conflict as a post-pubescent teenager in contending with a young woman who was so different from what their culture ascribed, especially in the 1950s. Only gradually did they begin to experience themselves together in a different way.

Another dimension of ambivalent attraction was understood as a manifestation of developmental conflicts in the transition from adolescence to early adulthood. Some individuals were wary of becoming involved in serious relationships when they were so unsure of themselves. For Douglas, his attraction to Della was as clear as any in our study:

What attracted me to Della was she was a nice built young lady, you know, nice hips and everything, heavy. She was a nice looking young woman. And I lived across the street from her, you know . . . . I used to see her come out on the porch and something was attractive to me. It's just the way she was built. She was just a nice looking young lady, very nice.

Della recalled that:

It was so funny. When I met him. . . . He had an aunt that lived across the street from us. . . . He was a very, very shy person . . . I don't think he knew that much about girls himself, OK. And he got involved with coming over to my mother's house, and he was so helpful; he's always been that type of person. He used to help me carry the water and everything. But my mother used to tell him: "What are you looking at my girls for?" And he'd just sit there and laugh, but my mother felt like he liked one of us, you know. And I was just praying to God that it wasn't me. Because I had no interest in him at all. He was just a boy. And I think at that time I didn't have any real interest in nobody, in nothing. I was just my mother's youngest daughter. He and I started going out with each other. And I still couldn't make up my mind that this is who I wanted to be with. I'm always curious about different things in life and I'll give it a shot, you know. So after I couldn't get him interested in . . . " Don't you want my sister? You don't like her?" "Don't you want my friend? She likes you a lot, you know." He used to just laugh at me. So finally he and I started to really go out with each other. At first, I don't think he and I was really even attracted to one another.

One may wonder about the messages, both overt and covert, which this young woman was picking up from this young man. Her mother certainly had no difficulty reading his agenda. Della's ambivalence was probably kept alive by several conflicting dynamics: her emerging sense of sexuality, her questions about her self-confidence, her mother's protectiveness, and Douglas's unambiguous sexual attraction to her.

SEXUAL ATTRACTION

Adams (1979) found that sexual attraction preceded other types of attraction. He further suggested that "physical impressions served primarily as screening devices during courtship" (p. 259). Physical attraction was a central dimension of the beginnings of relationships for most individuals in our study, although not everyone talked about its importance in the same way. Rarely was physical attraction expressed in isolation from other psychosocial attributes that played an equal or more influential role in bringing a couple together and in sustaining a relationship. Sooner or later intrinsic qualities in the other person which were attractive to an individual became essential to the survival of the relationship.

Although initial attraction was not differentiated stereotypically by gender, sexual attractiveness was mentioned by men more frequently than by women. Men used almost three times as many bodily grounded terms in recalling what initially attracted them to their future spouses. Sometimes, the memories were nonspecific yet clearly sexual as with Joseph, a 57-year-old college-educated, Jewish husband married thirty-two years:

> It was just one of those things when you met and you knew there were sparks flying and we just hit it off. That was it.

Most of the time, men were more specific than Joseph. Kevin, a 52-year-old college-educated Catholic married twenty-nine years, said simply:

> Her shape physically.

Women, on the other hand, spoke frequently of intrinsic qualities of a nonsexual nature which attracted them to their future spouse. Kate, the wife of Kevin, recalled that

> We started out as friends. We took a course together and started to talk. I liked his personality, mostly who he was; kind, good, happy and full of life ...

liked to have a good time, always laughing. I think I accepted him for who he was as a person. I did not have any prefixed notions.

Men became attracted to and valued psychosocial qualities as relationships evolved. Women, on the other hand, were more likely to recall being attracted to those qualities in men from the beginnings of relationships. More than any other quality, humor was mentioned by women. Men rarely mentioned humor in women as something that attracted them.

Shared values and a positive reaction to psychological characteristics, such as kindness and thoughtfulness, became important in sustaining the relationship. We found that the attractiveness of one to the other shifted frequently from bodily characteristics to intrinsic ones. Earl, a 53-year-old white Protestant married twenty-eight years, talked about his initial sexual response to his future spouse and how that changed as the relationship developed:

I think physically, she is a very attractive woman. The animal magnetism. I'm sure that's more important to a male than to a female. I was very attracted to her. That is the first instance, but also has to have some brain power behind it because after the honeymoon is over you have to talk and the physical attraction was important but not that important. Physical attraction and the quality of who she was as an individual.

The memories of Evelyn, Earl's wife, were quite different:

His sincerity and enthusiasm. The fact that I thought he would be a real steady person, not like some of the guys with the big minds that I had known. I knew it was it because I could not stand to be away from him. I felt alive, like I had found my second half. I just knew. I had to call my parents because our relationship was moving so fast.

The memories of these two people represented the responses of most men and women. Men were more likely to be attracted initially by their perceptions of physical characteristics and women by psychosocial ones. These observations were similar to the findings of other researchers (Margolin & White, 1987; Sprecher, 1989).

When sexual attraction was recalled by women, it was not that different from the memories of men except in one respect. Not only was it expressed as part of her overall attraction to her future spouse, but also it was sometimes framed within the context of other dynamics that she experienced. For example, Ann recalled her physical attraction to Andrew and then reflected on the meaning of what she perceived, at the time, as his rejection of her:

> You'll think I'm crazy but it was his curly hair! It was. He had hair that was like Huckleberry Finn's. It was all little curls and for some reason or other, well isn't that silly, yeah for some reason or other I just loved the curls on his head and wish he had them today. Although he looks as though he has. Would you believe it! Nuts! But that's what attracted me to him. And when he was younger I thought he was a little gruff, if you understand what I mean. When I look back on it now ... I was young ... from 15 to whatever. And I think they [boys] were, at that time, not able to say: "I really don't want a girl" and they don't even know why they like her. You understand what I mean. Truly, they're like that, and I think that they'd rather be with their gang of boys ... what is this girl doing to my head. I realized that afterward, many years afterward but at the time I was hurt. I supposed he didn't like me as much as I liked him.

This 72-year-old Irish Catholic woman married to Andrew for 47 years was reflecting on the narcissistic wounds of an adolescent in love and feeling rejected by the object of her love. This was one example of the many insights that both men and women shared with us during these interviews. While sexuality may have been central to the beginnings of marriage, psychosocial qualities such as empathic understanding became increasingly important as time passed. Each couple negotiated the balance among biological, psychological, and social dimensions in their own ways.

SYMMETRICAL ATTRACTION

Some individuals were attracted to one another because of characteristics that they had in common. In this study, couples were recruited because they had many similarities: race, ethnicity, religion, and socio-educational characteristics. By design, we included blacks, each of whom came from an African-American family background; Latinos, each of whom came from a Mexican-American family background; Jews who were married to other Jews; and blue-collar couples in which the principal wage earner may have had post–high school education but was not a college graduate. Thus, practically all spouses shared characteristics found to be instrumental in attracting individuals to one another (Robertson, 1987). Homogamous relationships by race, ethnicity, religion, and social status were reinforced by societal and family networks (Parks, Stan, & Eggert, 1983).

Geographic proximity fostered contact between people who had many demographic and other characteristics in common. Spatial closeness facilitated friendships between males and females which led to marriage (Kahn & McGaughy, 1977). Coupled with homogamous variables, proximity had a powerful effect on initial attraction. This was clearly the case among several Mexican Americans. Gonzalo, married for twenty-nine years to Guadalupe, recalled the first time that he noticed her:

> One day . . . we stopped to talk to some girls and one of those girls was Guadalupe and I asked if she thought I could see her again next week and she said sure so we sort of hit it off like that. I kind of saw her as the quiet person, the quiet type. She wasn't like other girls, you know that you would call them over to the car, and there they are, you know. But I don't know what it was about Guadalupe. Maybe God had a plan for us and I think about that a lot . . . God did have a plan back then and maybe he was trying to make me realize that Guadalupe was going to be my woman and that we were for each other and we were going to go through hard times and we were going to make it . . . thanks be to God, next year we'll celebrate our twenty-ninth anniversary, but it was just the way that she was, her own special way because she was just a little country girl.

Interestingly, Guadalupe was attracted to similar qualities in Gonzalo:

> Quietness. He was a very quiet person and had this look of sincerity in his eyes. When I see Gonzalo I see this innocence in his eyes. I guess that's why.

Burgess et al. (1954) observed that "commonality is rarely decisive in leading people to fall in love" (p. 100), yet it may set the stage for the process to begin, as it did for Gonzalo and Guadalupe. Their memories also illustrated the importance of symmetry in psychological characteristics. Each seemed to have been looking for a mate who would mirror qualities within themselves. We all feel safe in relationships, especially intimate relationships, with those with whom we experience a sense of mutual empathy and understanding. Homogamy may nurture that feeling.

Sometimes a sense of connection with someone else was facilitated and reinforced by mutual friends as it was for Donald and Doreen, both in their sixties and married forty years. They were Catholics and met in college. He said that

> It is hard to describe what attracted me to her. You feel comfortable with the person. You have a sense "here is a person with great integrity," someone with your values. It did not have an emotional "WOW." It was just the logic

of it and the fact that she wanted me and the fact that my good friends knew her before me. You don't rationalize these things, they just happen.

Doreen remembered that their meeting was arranged through

Recommendations from good friends. Something of mystery and difference, energy, interesting. Common interests, friends, outdoors, activeness. We both liked to be outdoors. The same things attracted him to me. I was different than other people he met, energy. The fact that we had mutual friends that put us together.

Implicit in the attraction between these people was a symmetry in underlying values which gave meaning and direction to their lives. Catholicism was such a resource for Donald and Doreen as well as Gonzalo and Guadalupe. For Debra and Daniel, values grounded in their Judaism were a central force in bringing and keeping them together:

We were fixed up by his sister ... so she arranged a blind date, and we met. Well, he was quite nice looking and, pleasant ... to be honest, I wasn't all that impressed. My mother thought he was wonderful. We had a lot of the same background in terms of family and the type home that we were brought up in. Both sets of parents were European-born Jews. And we just seemed to have a nice time. We seemed to have the same values. I don't know. Knowing someone and getting engaged was the thing to do at the time. I think our values brought us together more than our interests because as it turns out, we really don't have a lot of interests in common. We have a lot of values in common.

Several individuals spoke to the importance of similar values in attracting them to their future spouse. Symmetry in values may have facilitated mutuality of understanding and an acceptance of the other person. Connection of that sort may have resulted in a high level of positive feeling toward the spouse as well as a strong personal investment in the marriage (Cahn, 1983).

Finally, symmetry produced a unique relationship in which one experienced a sense of connection and kinship not present in any other relationship. Louis and Lilly expressed that thought as they talked with us about their initial attraction to each other. They had been married thirty-eight years. Both were Catholic; he was a college graduate and she had some college. Louis remembered that

> She was a very attractive girl, woman. I think the other thing of special interest, you could talk to her about almost anything. We had a lot in common. I would say initially, I just found her very attractive. That is usually the initial thing for a lot of men, physical attraction.

For Lilly, the meaning of being with Louis progressed rapidly to being with a kindred soul:

> It happened so fast. Actually, he was someone else's date. I met him on a bus. He was the roommate of this fellow that I had a date with. The friend said, "Could you fix Louis up with someone?" I said, "Sure." I fixed him up with my best friend at the time. My best friend decided she liked my date; she was hanging all over him. Louis and I were dancing. He said, "Why don't we leave here and go someplace else because they will never miss us?" So we did, we went for a walk and wound up at some little pub. Since then, we were never apart. It was just an instant recognition of a kindred soul. We started talking and never stopped.

Similarities were critical to couples getting together. Symmetry nurtured a sense of connectedness and mutuality which acted as glue in sustaining the relationship, especially through difficult times. In the last section of this chapter, we explore the flip side of symmetry, which is complementarity.

COMPLEMENTARY ATTRACTION

The Latin root of the word "complementarity" is *complementum*, which means to fill out or to complete. Whereas symmetrical qualities in other people resonated with and reinforced similiar qualities within one's sense of self, complementary qualities were different and had the perceived effect of making the self more complete. In other words, individuals were attracted to those whom they perceived as having attributes that were lacking in themselves (Honeycutt, 1986).

Exchange theory plays to the theme of complementarity in marital relationships. That is, individuals were likely to be attracted to potential mates whom they perceived as meeting their unfilled needs, which may have offered them an opportunity to experience fulfillment as an individual. Particular traits were valued and experienced as rewarding within a relationship. The exchange was mutually beneficial and provided each person with rewards not available outside of the relationship.

Felicidad recalled how she was attracted to Francisco. A Mexican-American couple, they had been married twenty-six years. It was interesting that her attraction to him was, to a considerable extent, illusionary. That is, Felicidad was responding to the role that Francisco had adopted in order to foster her attraction to him. He talked of his attraction to Felicidad:

> I was attracted to her immediately. . . . It seemed that there was an attraction to me too. It was subtle, but I played the shy one, you know, I didn't want to be overwhelming as it were, like "How about you and me" ... I was laid back.

Felicidad spoke of what was happening within herself as a result of meeting and being with Francisco:

> His shyness, his innocence, very good looking. I was used to guys coming on to me and he wasn't that way. . . . I wasn't afraid to talk to him. I remember being very active, very talkative and I think that, like they say, opposites attract. I think that he liked me for my personality, maybe ... I had had a lot of different relationships. I had been engaged like four or five times at the age of 15, but with him, it was like we belong together. He was home. Wherever he was, that was home to me. I tell people this and I really mean it. I was born when I met him. That's when I really started enjoying life. That's when I really started having fun. He was my all. He was all I wanted in life. I had had a hard childhood and misery was part of my life, and I didn't know that there was something so good.

Women were more likely than men to talk from their souls as Felicidad did. In part, that may have reflected the prevailing mores of an era when women were expected to be deferential to men. Perhaps, Felicidad felt that way because it was magnified by her personal history which included extreme poverty, neglect, and abandonment. We also know that women value relatedness and connection within a meaningful relationship in ways that are different from men. They may be more comfortable in talking in relational terms and feel less vulnerable in disclosing their inner selves which they may experience as incomplete outside of a meaningful relationship. This was mirrored in the memories of other women whom we have already met in this chapter. For example, Evelyn said that she had found her second half after she met Earl, her future husband. With Francisco we saw him talking at the periphery of the self—playing a role—while Felicidad spoke of what was happening within herself. As their stories unfolded, men spoke increasingly of their inner selves, especially as they negotiated middle and old age with the women whom they had fallen in love with years ago.

Complementary elements in initial attraction were often associated with developmental experiences in the family of origin. This was especially true when individuals were seeking a mate who may have shared the characteristics of an important role model and yet did not replicate their liabilities. Judy, a 56-year-old mother of six and married thirty-five years, expressed that need:

I guess the difference. My mother was always dragging me to the Hibernian Hall to meet Irish boys ... I just liked him from the beginning. He was different. He was different from my father because he was quiet and strong, and he wouldn't let me push him around. So, that attracted me.

Her husband recalled:

I liked the way she made me feel, I liked the way we got along together.

A part of initial attraction, based on one's perception of differences, was often related to issues of self-esteem. In a potential spouse, individuals with low self-esteem may have sought those qualities which they felt were lacking within themselves (Mathes & Moore, 1985). Ken was attracted to Karen because she was "very pretty and very shapely." She was attracted to him because he had a "great personality and a fabulous sense of humor," and:

He was very confident ... I just liked ... that part of him; he seemed to have things under control all the time, you know.... I never felt that I was a person that stood out in the crowd. Oh I was popular in high school, I was elected most popular, I was a cheerleader and that, but I was not in the real big clique, and I never considered myself as someone who was outstanding. I think I was attractive, but I was never confident. I don't know what attracted him to me.

Implicit in several of these examples was the influence of expected gender roles in initial attraction. Given the prevailing mores of the era which ascribed different marital roles for husbands and wives, one might have expected more explicit reference to this variable than was found. Although there was a subtle theme of men being attracted to women who were vulnerable yet nurturing and women to men who were strong and protective, this was not a pervasive memory among respondents. The variability in responses may have been related to the diversity of our sample. The research on this subject supported that explanation. On the one hand, people have been found to be attracted to potential spouses who have traditional sex roles (Orlofsky, 1982); on the other hand, other studies have suggested that individuals are attracted by the perception of androgynous roles (Lombardo, Francis, & Brown, 1988).

SUMMARY

Seventy-eight percent of the individuals in this study were attracted positively to their future spouses. Twenty-two percent of the participants who reported not being attracted positively were predominantly women who were initially ambivalent about the men whom they would marry. African-American women reported more ambivalence than other women. Variability in the nature of initial attraction suggests that this phenomenon was complex for both sexes and best framed within a biopsychosocial perspective. Physical, psychological, and social dynamics fueled the attraction of one person to another in ways that were unique for each couple. Compared to women, men were initially attracted by physical attributes and women by psychosocial ones. Even among men, sexual attraction was a prelude to attraction grounded on intrinsic psychological attributes. Among a few individuals, the decision to marry was made spontaneously at the time of the first encounter with the person who would become their future spouse. For most people, the commitment to marry was made after several months or years of courtship. Finally, interpersonal attraction was sustained by the interplay of symmetrical and complementary qualities perceived in the other person. Similarities or having something in common seemed to have nurtured attachment to the loved one, while differences of a complementary nature offered one a sense of personal fulfillment.

REFERENCES

Adams, B. (1979). Mate selection in the United States: A theoretical summarization. In W. R. Burr, R. Hill, F. I. Nye, & I. Reiss (Eds.). *Contemporary theories about the family* (pp. 259–267). New York: Free Press.

Burgess, E., Wallin, P., & Schultz, G. (1954). *Courtship, engagement and marriage.* Philadelphia: J. P. Lippincott.

Cahn, D. D. (1983). Relative importance of perceived understanding in initial interaction and development of interpersonal relationships. *Psychological Reports, 52,* 923–929.

Givens, P. B. (1978). Nonverbal basis of attraction. *Psychiatry, 41* (4), 346–359.

Honeycutt, J. M. (1986). A model of marital functioning based on an attraction paradigm and social-penetration dimensions. *Journal of Marriage and the Family, 48,* 651–667.

Kahn, A. & McGaughy, T. (1977). Distance and closeness: When moving close produces increased likeness. *Sociometry, 40* (2), 138–144.

Lombardo, J., Francis, P., & Brown, S. (1988). Sex role and opposite sex interpersonal attraction. *Perceptual and Motor Skills, 67,* 855–869.

Margolin, L. & White, L. (1987). The continuing role of physical attractiveness in marriage. *Journal of Marriage and the Family, 49,* 21–27.

Mathes, E. W., & Moore, C. L. (1985). Reik's complementarity theory of romantic love. *Journal of Social Psychology, 125* (3), 321–327.

Moore, M., & Butler, D. (1989). Predictive aspects of nonverbal courtship in women. *Semiotica, 76* (3–4), 205–212.

Orlofsky, J. (1982). Psychological androgyny, sex typing and sex role ideology as predictors of male-female initial attraction. *Sex Roles, 8*(10).

Parks, M., Stan, C., & Eggert, L. (1983). Romantic involvement and social network involvement. *Social Psychology Quarterly, 46* (2), 116–131.

Pinderhughes, E. (1989). *Understanding race, ethnicity and power: Key to efficacy in clinical practice.* New York: Free Press.

Robertson, I. (1987). *Sociology.* New York: Worth Publishers.

Sprecher, S. (1989). The importance to males and females of physical attractiveness, earning potential, and expressiveness in initial attraction. *Sex Roles, 21* (9/10), 591–607.

—2—

Relationship

... no marriage is perfect, and no marriage is without conflict ... I
think we have learned to live with and accept each other ...

During the decades in which these couples married (1940s, 1950s, and
1960s), marital roles were ascribed more than they are today. Even then,
however, modes of being in a relationship had to be negotiated either
directly by discussion or indirectly by the ways individuals behaved with
one another. In other words, gender roles were based on ascriptions of
expected behaviors by sex as well as on how individuals experienced
themselves and behaved within relationships. These two dynamics were
central to the quality of marital relationships from their beginnings, through
the parenting years, and into the post-parenting years.

Changes in marriage were taking place during those decades, although
the predominant mode of role relations in marriage was of a traditional
nature. In their survey of marriages from 1964 to 1974, Mason and Bumpass
(1975) found a shift occurring toward egalitarian roles within marriage
along with continuity in differentiation of roles by gender. That is, gradual
changes in the direction of integrating instrumental and expressive behav-

iors in marriage were happening, but the predominant expectations were for women to take on the roles of homemaker, and mother and, in terms of the marital relationship, to defer to the authority of husbands. In contrast, husbands were expected to be the head of households, to work outside the home in order to support the family, and to provide for its security. In this differentiation of roles by gender, women were defined by their expressive behaviors in nurturing and being sensitive to others within relationships and men by their instrumental behaviors as breadwinners.

This chapter explores how individuals experienced themselves and their spouses within the context of marital relationships. We begin with their expectations of marriage: the roles that they saw themselves and their spouse playing in the relationship as well as how marital roles evolved over the years. The discussion is based on the idea of understanding marital role behaviors along a continuum. Expressive behaviors characterize one pole and instrumental behaviors the other pole; task-centered behaviors were classified as instrumental and relationship behaviors as expressive. Pure types were more characteristic of role expectations than of actual behaviors throughout marriage. That is, most respondents entered marriage with the expectation of assuming traditional roles in their relationships. Prior to the birth of the first child, men described their role behaviors as instrumental, while women recalled their role behaviors as being more expressive. The realities of being married, especially after children were born, led to changes and a greater integration of instrumental and expressive dimensions in men.

The second section of this chapter focuses on the fit of one spouse with the other. This extends the discussion beyond the classification of roles in the first section to examine specific modes of relatedness. In marriage people may fit together in several different ways. Watzlawick, Beavin, and Jackson (1967) proposed that relationships may be symmetrical to complementary, depending as much on internal signals as they do on the perception of the other person. Complementary relationships are based on differences and symmetrical ones on similarities. It is the sense of difference to similarity as well as equality to inequality which defines the symmetrical to complementary nature of relationships. Complementary relationships are experienced as fulfilling the self and symmetrical relationships as reinforcing the self.

The third focus is on relational values: trust, respect, sensitivity, and understanding. These variables were selected after a review of the literature which included scholarly as well as popular articles and books. Throughout the literature, these four qualities were repeatedly identified as important in marital stability and happiness. Therefore, we asked individuals to tell us about these qualities both in terms of observations of their own behaviors and of their spouse's behaviors.

The chapter concludes with an examination of communication patterns throughout the three phases of marriage. Marital communication has probably been studied more than any other variable. The fit of spouses within marriage, ego with alter ego, is negotiated by way of communication. Optimal communication requires a grounding in mutual values of trust, respect, sensitivity, and understanding. As with other foci in this chapter, we explored how communication may have been shaped by gender, ethnicity, educational level, and religion.

ROLES: EXPECTATIONS

Most individuals entered marriage with clearly differentiated expectations of marital roles which mirrored prevailing cultural mores about "appropriate" behaviors for men and women during that era. Nine out of ten people expressed little ambiguity in recalling expectations of themselves in the marital relationship. Gender was not related significantly to role expectations. Men defined themselves primarily in terms of work so as to provide for their families; women, in terms of supporting their husbands and taking care of their families. There was an implicit power differential in these memories which was sometimes stated explicitly.

Expectations of self and spouse were shaped by experiences in the family of origin. People frequently referred to role models with whom they identified. These mental representations of what it was like to be a husband and wife served as transitional resources as people thought of their roles in marriage. Grover, a 53-year-old college graduate married thirty-one years, wished

> To see myself as the professional breadwinner of the family. Gladys was going to be the homemaker, and we were going to have kids. She would take care of them, and that was going to be our life. That is the way I saw it. That is how I was brought up. At the time, my mother was working, but when I was a kid, she was a homemaker. I kind of modeled that that was what marriage was gonna be.

Gladys, 50 years of age and a high school graduate, spoke of her expectations as being part of herself from a young age. The concept of becoming a wife was grounded in her identification with a mother who, like herself, worked outside the home:

My mom was a typical housewife, even though she worked. Her husband and family came first. I was brought up to feel that my family came first. From the time I was a little girl I wanted to grow up and get married. That was my goal in life. I wanted to be a mom and wife. I expected to stay home and raise my family. That is pretty much what happened. I have been very fortunate, I have everything in life that I have ever turned out to want ... I expected Grover to be ... the breadwinner, the supporter, mentally, physically, and every other way. The leaning tower in any part but still the person I could lean on. The stronger of the two of us. That is very much how it worked out and still is today.

These memories were representative of those individuals whose expectations were of a traditional nature. Among African Americans, however, a trend was found toward expecting nontraditional roles. Carol, a 51-year-old African-American woman, spoke to that theme. Clearly, Carol, married for thirty-three years, expected the relationship with Carl to be

Equal, cause I had seen too many of my friends and my own mother in the circumstances that I was not going to put up with in any way, form, shape or fashion. And so that was it from day one and he knew it ... an equal role ... decision making and every aspect of married life, I felt, should entail the husband and wife together. And there were difficult days because he, as a man from the South, didn't operate on the same premise all the time like his father and uncle so it was a learning experience for both of us.

Carl talked of what he wanted from Carol:

Well, I saw it as a mother-to-be and just as a role of a regular housewife and listen to my problems if I had any and share in my life with her. ... So we both take part in that. It's not one person's sole responsibility ... I don't want her to just do everything towards the baby. I want to share in it too. I helped with the cooking and cleaning. We've always done that.

This couple reflected the differences that were found between African Americans and the other two ethnic groups. Twenty-five percent of the African Americans talked in nontraditional terms about their expectations compared to 3 percent of whites and 8 percent of the Mexican Americans $[X^2 (2, N = 120) = 11.62, p = .003]$. As with Carol, African-American women may not have wished to replicate what they had observed in the marriages of others. African Americans as well as Mexican Americans also expected that their marriages would require work and effort. Over half of Mexican Americans and African Americans compared to 30 percent of whites expected to work at their marriages [$X^2 (4, N = 120) = 9.42, p = .05$]. White couples did not see and, sometimes rejected, the question of loving relationships requiring effort in order to make them work. Perhaps because of racism and feelings of oppression, life was difficult for African Americans and Mexican Americans, including happiness in marriage, which could be realized only with significant effort. Nothing came easy. Although they had much in common with Mexican Americans, African Americans did not have the close connection to and involvement with their extended families. As a consequence, more stress and conflict were reported at the beginning of their marriages compared to others, and there was an expressed need to negotiate roles within their relationships.

Among Mexican Americans, expectations about gender roles in marriage were highly differentiated. The language of Mexican-American males was focused primarily on work as in the memories of Gonzalo:

Well, I knew that I would be the provider and I learned at a young age to go out in the world by myself and get a job. Thanks be to God, I started off at a very young age getting a job and I loved to work and once you're working, you know, you have at least money to feed your wife and your children and to help buy things that you need. So I learned that on my own, to go out and do for myself, not to depend on my mom and dad because I knew the situation they were in and that they couldn't help me out, so I had to learn the situation the hard way—go out there, and if I wanted to survive in the world for my wife and my kids, then I would have to have a job.

His wife, Guadalupe, recalled her expectations:

I knew that if I got married, I would have children, and I would have to take care of them ... through my mom and dad's marriage, there were seven of us and I knew that when mom left there was nobody to take care of us ... dad was there in a way; he never left us. But he had to go to work and come back and I said when I get married, I'll never leave my children like this. So I knew that if I was going to have children, I'd have to take care of those children ... I was very content to be at home and then it got to where we were having bill problems and I thought that this was my family and I should be able to help Gonzalo with the bills. The girls were still little. We had two girls and grandma would take care of them while I went out and worked.

In their expectations of self and of their future spouses, Jewish couples had much in common with Mexican-American couples, despite the fact that their levels of education and family income were the furthest apart of any two groups in the study. All Jewish respondents talked of their expectations in highly traditional terms compared to 92 percent of the Catholics and 82 percent of the Protestants [X^2 (2, $N = 120$) = 6.45, $p = .04$]. Brian and Bernice, a Jewish couple in their mid-sixties who had been married forty-three years, spoke to that theme:

> BRIAN: Probably at that time, the male dominant thing was more appropriate than it is now. I think I probably did more of the deciding about where to go and what to do. It was taken for granted in our generation that the man would work and the woman wouldn't. And as soon as I was able to make enough money so that we could live, Bernice left her job. And that was considered the right thing to do. Well, I mean, she actually left it when we had kids . . . it was assumed that she would never go back to work, but she did.

> BERNICE: I was very subservient . . . he probably sensed that he was the dominant one and I think that pleased him. We were at the stage in life where one stayed home and you were a housewife. Over the years we have grown to know that that isn't our role. My main role in life was to be a good wife. I really believed that . . . I wanted to get married, and I felt that my husband came first. My husband always came first . . . and he comes first now. My husband was my best friend, and he's my best friend now.

Expectations of self in marriage were shaped by several factors which are illustrated in the memories of these people. Family background and cultural values were central. This was evident in Gonzalo and Guadalupe in which the instrumental role for males and the nurturing role for women were ascribed from an early age. Those expectations had been internalized in highly syntonic ways. When individuals knew within themselves who they were to be in marriage and were not in conflict with that ascription, there may not have been as much need to negotiate marital roles with their future spouse. Mutual expectations congruent with roles modeled in the family of origin mitigated conflict as happened in the lives of Brian and Bernice.

When the cultural mores to which one was socialized in the family of origin conveyed a clear and unambiguous message under secure economic conditions, people entering marriage may not have needed to think of expending effort to make their relationships work. This was found among Jewish couples who were economically more secure than others. Compared to Catholics and Protestants, 77 percent of the Jewish respondents did not expect that much effort would be needed to make their marriages work [X^2 (4, $N = 120$) = 20.57, $p = < .001$]. On the one hand, relative economic security along with clear cultural expectations about marital roles may have resulted in people not even thinking about effort. On the other hand, poverty may have created stresses that undermined the romantic notion that love conquers all.

ROLES: REALITY

Despite the role expectations of respondents, their recollections of actual behaviors in marriage were quite different [X^2 (2, $N = 120$) = 17.72, $p = < .001$]. In describing their roles, 70 percent of the men talked predominantly of instrumental behaviors prior to the birth of the first child. Minimal references were made to expressive behaviors. Women, on the other hand, described their roles as more complex during the initial phase of marriage. Although one-third of women talked primarily in expressive terms, two-thirds used a mixture of instrumental and expressive words in recalling their roles, even if they did not work outside the home. For example, Barbara, a 57-year-old Catholic high school graduate who was married thirty-seven years, recalled that time and how her behavior changed:

> You always make sure that your man was happy and that your family's happy. I used to shine his shoes and my daughter's shoes every night . . . all these things that I don't do anymore. I think I was stupid. That was my upbringing that you do those things. I was only half of a person. I didn't demand anything. Everything was like clockwork . . . I worked . . . I had dinner on at six and nobody ever left without breakfast. Now it's totally different. Now I demand, if he gets up early: "You make the coffee, you make the breakfast." But I didn't do this before, so how could he respect me? He respected me but not as a person because I didn't demand it.

Among men, Art, a 64-year-old African-American father of seven children, reflected how most men recalled the two principal elements in their roles:

> I was the breadwinner and the head of the household, the head of the family, a strong head, based on the tradition that I was brought up with. I've seen a lot of studies, and they say that most of the black families are matriarchal. That might be true now; I don't know. But that was never true when I was growing up. The man was the head of the house, and that was no problem. There was no question about it. But nowadays, they're saying something else. But anyways, the tradition if you will, that I was raised with is that the man is the head of the family, no question. And that's what I did . . . I might be a bit chauvinistic maybe, but that's the way I've always done it.

During the second phase of marriage, child-rearing, a shift in marital roles was evident. During those years, 44 percent of the men began to integrate expressive dimensions into their roles which, in the first phase of marriage, had been described by 70 percent of the males in instrumental terms. Parenting, which required expressive as well as instrumental skills, was the reason for that shift. Among blue-collar couples, the process of change was often triggered by wives asking for help with the children. Andrew, a 72-year-old retired plumber, described how the change came about in his family:

> Well , I ... wasn't certainly a prima donna. I'd be happy to give her time; but when we had most of the child-rearing I was an apprentice and I didn't have much time to do anything, but I wouldn't hesitate ... Ann wouldn't think to ask you to change the diaper ... not that I didn't do it when she wasn't there but when she was there she felt it was her job. Not that I felt that it was, because lots of things I've always helped with whether it be the dishes or something ... with the children ... ah ... I was always there if needed. But she was the prime one to do anything.... If something had to be corrected it was done there by whoever. And there was no criticism on her part or my part over discipline. I guess you have the same values.

His spouse, Ann, mirrored Andrew's memories:

> You see he was very helpful. I have to laugh today that men need this bonding with their children. Any men I knew ... were always very involved with their children, involved with the house.... The world has changed that much, I know. But at the time, he was very helpful. Every Saturday I'd go shopping and he'd take care of these four children. I'd leave in the morning and go in and eat my lunch.... and shop around just for the day. No, he was very helpful and a wonderful father. I couldn't say that he wasn't. But ... every other man I knew was too.

While this shift in roles may be attributed to the demands of raising children, especially in their teenage years, it was related also to women becoming employed outside of the home which required more participation among men in parenting children. For middle-class women, employment was often part of their aspirations to combine career with motherhood; for working-class women, entry into the workforce was usually associated with the anticipation of children attending college and the need to generate more family income.

By the time the youngest child in these families had reached 18 and the parents were in transition to the "empty-nest" phase, the shift toward men becoming less instrumental and more expressive was evident among respondents as they talked of their relationships. Men used less instrumental and more expressive terms in describing themselves. Fifty-three percent of husbands talked in mixed or expressive terms about their marital roles. Although several women also became more expressive, the dramatic change occurred among men. Clearly, men regarded themselves in terms that were more relationally valued, which had been characteristic of most women throughout the marriage. Although the gender differences in role behaviors did not disappear in this post-parenting period [X^2 (2, N = 120) = 10.44, p = .001], they were less dramatic than in previous phases.

The process of change from the beginning of marriage to the present was described by Eve and Douglas. Change for Douglas was triggered by the chronic illness of his wife, Della. He responded by taking on new behaviors that were alien to him at the beginning of the marriage; he began by recalling his early expectations and then talked of how he had changed:

I knew that you got married and you had kids and the ... husband's supposed to be the boss and the leader, and all that kind of stuff. And the wife stays home and the man can go out and do anything he wants to do, and it's supposed to be OK ... I expected her to make sure that she had food cooked for me, and my clothes washed and clean, and that whatever I do is alright, ... she just keeps quiet. It was crazy, my thinking was then .... And now it's a little bit different ... I do all the cleaning up now. I'm the housewife now . .. I fix her breakfast, I bring her breakfast every morning in bed. And I bring her pills ... she's a diabetic, I bring her needle up. And whatever she wants done I do it. I vacuum the house, I do all the cleaning up around here now. I do the floors, I do everything. And I don't even mind it. It don't even bother me. But I did. I thought women did all those things. Men didn't do that; it was a woman's job. And that's the way I thought then. Today I don't think that way; today I do it.

Eve described the process of change in her marriage:

In the first phase I thought, Edward will grow out of it. He'll be a father when the first one's born.... And he didn't. Disappointment, I guess, for that one. In the second phase I felt rejected, overburdened, unloved and the third one, I feel loved ... we're sharing responsibilities. Like everything else, it's just come so far. It's really amazing to see it grow.... Maybe I wasn't assertive in the first part of the years ... now I feel more comfortable and confident that I can tell him what I want done and he can help me.... His values were awful in the beginning, and then they probably got a little better because you have the responsibility to the children; your values do have to change because you don't want your kids doing what their father's doing. I always have had high values, so my values have always been the same. Unfortunately, sometimes, you know, maybe they are too high, but that's what I believe in . . . . Edward's have come more to mine.

While the modification in the post-parenting structure depicted by these two people was, no doubt, influenced by outside events, such as retirement, the critical aspects appeared to be shaped substantially by transitions within marital relationships, which had begun in the child-rearing period, particularly during the adolescent years of children. Change was also shaped by illnesses that affected both spouses. Medical crises were a turning point. For Eve and Douglas, crises brought about a new manifestation of love not previously evident in their relationship with their spouses.

INTERPERSONAL FIT: COMPLEMENTARITY TO SYMMETRY

In marriage interpersonal fit may be thought of along a continuum from complementarity to symmetry. Complementary styles of relating were characterized by differences in marital behavior, division of tasks, decision-making, child-rearing, and emotional responses to each other. Given the cultural mores about gender roles when these people were married, we expected their relationships to be of a complementary nature. Indeed, 78 percent of the respondents spoke initially in complementary terms about their relationships, a finding that did not change significantly from the beginnings of marriage to the empty-nest years, with a slight shift toward symmetry during the latter phase. If spouses discussed their relationships in language that reflected similarities and equality, the fit was considered symmetrical. That style was evident in the response of a middle-class woman who said that she and her husband were much alike emotionally, enjoyed similar things, and generally made mutual decisions. Three out of ten respondents talked of their relationships as having both symmetrical and complementary features in the final phase, and the fit was classified as mixed.

Complementarity was manifested in two principal ways: personal traits perceived in self and spouse which were not always gender related; that is, men were not always dominant and women submissive. Behavior(s) based on levels of psychosocial development was another source of complementarity. A complementary theme was evident in the relationship of Ben and Barbara. He spoke about his perception of their personality traits:

> I consider myself as rather reserved, and she is outgoing ... she makes friends automatically and immediately. I am not that way ... it takes me a while to get close to people ... and she has made our marriage much easier by her being the way she is.

In discussing the relationship, Barbara talked of how developmental experiences shaped the fit between her and Ben. Her selective understanding of his early upbringing brought meaning to their relationship, which allowed for acceptance of differences and recognition of strengths:

> Ben is really very fair ... and very lovable, but he can't show it. But that is not his fault ... it was his upbringing. If you dig long enough you get everything out of him ... at times he is like a little kid. He is a good husband, but his needs are different ... he missed some of it growing up and he is looking for it now. He is a very kind man ... and I usually get what I need from him.

Francisco, who was from a Mexican background, discussed developmental and trait differences in the following way:

> We are opposites. She's over here as the strong decision-making disciplinarian type person. I'm over here and I want to have fun. I'm still a teenager. ... There's nothing serious in my life. And we complement each other. She keeps things in order, making sure everything goes right, and I get the fun part of it.

His spouse, Felicidad, offered the following observations:

> He's understanding of me and my problems and background. His supportiveness in everything that I wanted to do or not to do, his patience ... I'm very fortunate.

Couples who had different personality traits talked about differences bringing a balance to their relationships. John described complementary aspects of his relationship with Judy:

> I am not as outspoken. I'm a lot quieter. Like I said, one's a talker, and one's a listener. That helps a lot. She's a reader. I'm more of a doer. I always envied her for being able to read, I always wished I could.

Judy saw it this way:

He will always be an athlete before he's a play-goer or a movie-goer. I tend
to go to plays. I love to read and do movies ... I am a risk-taker and he thinks
things out very carefully ... I wish he wasn't as careful. But maybe the balance
is what works.

Building a relationship based on complementarity was a reciprocal
process. In responding to the spouse, whether those needs be grounded in
traits, developmental differences, or both, individuals also experienced a
fulfillment of their own needs. Perhaps the stability of complementarity was
related to fundamental qualities within the selves of each spouse which were
not likely to change as relationships matured.

A sizable minority of spouses (30 percent) perceived both symmetrical
and complementary qualities in their relationships. Most often, people
spoke to a mutuality of values and goals along with differences in traits.
David and Donna were such a couple. David reported that

We can argue about an item, but I think our basic values are very close to
each other ... as far as the goals of our moral thoughts I think they are very
close. However, I am volatile and she is still a peacemaker.

Symmetry in relationships was evident in the observations of the following two couples. Kevin and Kate, one of the youngest couples in our study
at 51 years of age, used symmetrical language in describing their relationship. Kevin observed:

We have sharing in the relationship. We like to go out and shop, like to be
busy ... We like to eat out. A lot of compatibility. She liked to do those things.
It was real compatibility ... in life and in bed.

In responding to the same question in her interview, Kate said:

What really kept us together is that we believe in each other. We look
forward to spending our lives together. We have so much fun. The dumbest
things we can have the best time doing. Taking a walk. I think I have raised
his sights as to where he thought he could go and who he is as a person ... we
just keep growing and reaching, but never too high that we lose sight of
where we are going ... we never set anything so high that it is impossible to
reach.

Symmetry was reflected in common interests and in perceptions of
mutuality as in the marriage of Louis and Lilly who had been married
thirty-eight years. Louis discussed sharing common interests:

We both came from families where there were unhappy marriages. That was one thing we had in common. I had read a lot, and she had read a lot. I don't remember all the things we discussed, but it was always interesting.

Lilly spoke of mutuality:

We talked about books that we read, school experiences, life experiences … we never lacked things to talk about, we had read a lot of the same books. To me the most important thing is that I feel I have been blessed. I am very lucky to have met someone that is like a kindred spirit. It is like living with your best friend all the time. Being together. Everything is just great when you are with someone that you get along with so well.

RELATIONAL VALUES: SENSITIVITY, UNDERSTANDING, RESPECT, AND TRUST

The study included an examination of a cluster of variables referred to as relational values. Researchers (Chodorow, 1978; Gilligan, 1982; Surrey, 1984) have described gender roles as observable at an early age, hypothesizing that socialization and development create differences in the psychological makeup of men and women. Men have an agentic orientation; that is, they value achievement, autonomy, self-assertion, and self-expansion. Women have a communal orientation and are concerned about interpersonal relationships, affiliation, and interdependence and are more relational in their styles of marital interaction.

Self-in-relation theory emphasizes the centrality of attachments and interpersonal connections in the lives of women. The "relational self," the core self-structure in women, frames their values about connectedness with others. Therefore, women may have put their efforts into preserving harmony and connection in marriage while men focused on independence and achievement. Our explorations of relational values supported research on gender differences as those differences were played out between spouses.

Throughout the three stages of marriage, husbands viewed wives as being more sensitive and understanding than themselves; wives saw themselves also as more sensitive and understanding than their husbands. These significant findings ($p = < .05$) resonated with previous research on gender. That is, husbands viewed wives as sensitive and understanding. The converse was also true: wives viewed husbands as not very sensitive and understanding. In terms of trust and respect there were no significant gender differences. These two qualities were highly valued and did not change appreciably from the beginning of marriages through the empty-nest years.

Although similar patterns were found when individuals talked of how sensitive, understanding, trusting, and respectful they were toward their spouses, some variations were found. Husbands valued personal understanding toward their wives in much the same way as women did toward them. However, husbands did not value personal sensitivity as highly as wives.

College graduates and noncollege graduates differed in their respect for their spouses. During the early years and extending into the parenting phase, college graduates reported higher levels of respecting their spouses than did noncollege graduates ($p = < .05$). These differences disappeared by the post-parenting phase. When individuals were asked how much they thought their spouses trusted them, a difference was found by level of education. Three out of four noncollege graduates and almost all college graduates saw themselves as trustworthy during the first two phases of marriage ($p = < .01$).

Trusting one's spouse and being trusted by the spouse were different depending on ethnic group. Although a majority of respondents reported mutual trust in their relationships, the level of trust in one's spouse as well as the perception of how much the spouse trusted the respondent remained relatively constant throughout marriage among white couples. African Americans reported more conflict with mutual trust than others ($p = < .01$). Trusting one's spouse during the parenting years was more of an issue than at any other period, especially among Mexican-American couples. By the empty-nest years, differences between ethnic groups were still reported, but the groups looked more alike than different.

No significant trends emerged from the data by religion except in one area. Trusting in one's spouse was valued more by Catholics and Jews than by Protestants ($p = < .05$). Although that theme was found throughout the three phases of marriage, trusting the spouse was less differentiated by religion during the parenting years.

Despite these differences, the trend over the three phases of marriage was toward an enhancement of mutual trust, respect, understanding, and sensitivity. It appeared that trust and respect were fundamental to marital stability and an indispensable dimension of marital structure. Sensitivity and understanding were critical to stability and structure but changed more noticeably than did respect and trust. Perhaps sensitivity and understanding were developed as spouses adapted to one another over the years, while trust and respect were so inherently a part of marital structure from the beginning that they did not change as much. In other words, values of a trusting and respectful nature may have been a part of individuals when they married. The stability of trust and respect throughout marriage may have been the basis on which understanding and sensitivity toward the spouse were learned, nurtured, and internalized.

Sensitivity

In considering sensitivity to the needs of their wives over the years of the marriage, husbands reported they were not as sensitive to their wives as wives were to them. Frequently, men talked of how preoccupation with their careers may have undermined sensitivity. For example, Joseph, a 57-year-old Jewish executive married for thirty-two years, said:

> I am not as sensitive as I should be. There are times when I get preoccupied with my own thoughts and problems around a possible loss of my career. I was very insensitive, and she was very sensitive and supportive.

Several men expressed a sense of struggling to be sensitive toward their spouses, which was quite different from how women talked about sensitivity. Harold, a 56-year-old African-American tradesman, married for thirty-seven years with five children, observed:

> I tried to be sensitive. I know that she is a little more sensitive than I am. I try to be as much as possible.

The reports of women about the sensitivity of their husbands mirrored how men viewed themselves. The observations of wives about husbands changed as marriages entered the empty-nest years. Both spouses reported increased sensitivity among husbands in those years. Even then, however, men were often perceived as having difficulty with sensitivity. Cora, a 66-year-old woman with three children, had this observation about her husband:

> I do not think that this is one of his highest scoring areas. But I feel that is the way he is. He would never be nasty or unkind, but I don't think he is the most sensitive person in the world.

More than at any other time, women expressed disappointment with their husbands' lack of sensitivity during the child-rearing years. Karen, a 51-year-old working mother of four, shared these memories:

> I think that men are not as sensitive. My husband is sensitive in many ways ...but I think there were times where he has been insensitive with the raising

of the children and with me, and the things that I have done ... his least sensitive stage was the second stage with the children.

The change in sensitivity among men was reflected in what Isaac, a 56-year-old businessman married for twenty-nine years with two grown children, observed:

As far as being sensitive to what she was going through at that point in time and what she needed, I lacked a bit of that ... now I think it's on a pretty even keel.

Understanding

Spousal levels of understanding were similar to patterns found in sensitivity. Although both spouses described an increase in mutual understanding, husbands felt more understood by wives throughout the marriage than the other way around. The change in understanding of husbands, especially during the post-parenting years, was illustrated in the observations of Judy, a 56-year-old working mother with six children:

I think it is something that evolved over the years. I don't think that we really knew each other at the beginning, and I don't think he really understood me in those younger years ... the frustrations of child bearing and raising children. I think it is something he learned ... it's very hard to be free and easy, and then have all of this responsibility. I think that it's just as hard for a man in his own way, and I understood that. I think we have grown to understand each other a lot better.

From the perspective of husbands, change was viewed in the following manner by Guy, an African-American husband:

We got to understand each other as time went by, and we accepted each other more instead of trying to change the other one.

Selective understanding of spouses was a strategy employed by many individuals to adapt in their marriages. By developing awareness of the connections between family background and marital behaviors, adaptation to the spouse was possible. An example of this strategy was described by Kirsten who had been married for over fifty years:

I understand a lot of things about him that I don't think he gives me credit for. And a lot of things I have looked on as I have matured. I can understand where he came from because of the family that he comes from. And I can understand why he is like he is, because I don't think he had the relationship with his dad that he should have. And so it goes down. If he didn't have it, he don't have it to give. And I think that has a lot to do with how he is at times.

A small minority of husbands expressed reservations about the level of understanding of their wives. For example, Corey, a retired African-American man, commented:

Well, myself, I think I understand her pretty good, as far as understanding her condition, and her mind and what not. I'm not so sure that she understands me so good.

Respect

Respect is crucial in maintaining a stable marriage (Barnes & Buss, 1985; Lewis & Spanier, 1979). Respondents valued mutual respect. As has been pointed out, there was little variation over time regarding how much respect spouses felt they gave and received from each other. This theme was expressed in a variety of ways. Ben, a 58-year-old laborer, married for thirty-seven years, said it simply:

I've always felt that she respected me.

Fran, a 61-year-old high school graduate with five children, echoed a similar sentiment:

He had great respect for me. I think that's one of his characters, that he wouldn't do anything I ever remembered that would hurt me in any way.

In a small number of relationships, respect developed over time; that was depicted by Jill, married thirty-seven years and the mother of four children:

I think he respected me pretty well after the children ... you know before it was just me and him. It was okay but it wasn't great. But when we started having these children, that was the first thing we had to learn, to have great respect for one another. You got to know that you got to draw the reins in now, you know. You're really beginning to be a family, and you got to have respect for one another.

Trust

Trust was the basis of stability in these marriages. It involved fidelity to one's spouse, the spirit of which was captured by Earl, a 53 year old who had been married for twenty-eight years:

That has been one hundred percent . . . no jealousy, no outside sexual relations ... always temptations. I just decided that I am not gonna fool around on the side and she has not either. We talk about this. We don't take each other for granted. We know how important it is to feel comfortable. If you have to worry about your wife fooling around or vice versa, that is so destructive . . . I wanted to marry someone you can trust and respect.

A few individuals had reservations about trusting their spouse. Those who reported difficulties with trust often referred to concerns about alcoholism or the potential for sexual affairs by the spouse. Jane, an African-American woman married for thirty-two years, recalled:

Well, there was always a little hesitation there because I know he had an eye for women. So I guess I didn't trust him completely, but I had nothing to base it on. So I just put it out of my head.

Among some Mexican Americans, trust in the sexual faithfulness of husbands became an issue after children were born. Fundamental to their concept of trust was fidelity to family. It was critical for wives to be able to count on the faithful availability of their husbands as central figures in the family, an idea that was expressed by Buena:

The whole essence to everything in our culture is family, our family, our children . . . I expect my husband to support me. Back up the family unit, always be there with family, a family figure, not just in words, but actually be there to participate in rearing the children. He had to participate in that . . . teach the boys to be boys, teach them skills . . . he had to take part in that family position.

COMMUNICATION OVERVIEW

There is no doubt that the quality of marriage is related to how spouses encode and decode messages about one another within the context of their relationships. Although marital communication involves many levels and dimensions of human interaction which occur simultaneously, most research has focused on different components such as the expression of affection and self-disclosure (Chelune, Rosenfeld, & Waring, 1985; Rosenfeld & Welsh, 1985), conflict resolution (Billings, 1979; Gottman, 1982), verbal skills (White et al., 1986), and nonverbal aspects (Noller, 1984).

We found communication to be a highly complex dynamic. Except for ethnicity, there was considerable uniformity among respondents about the quality of communication from the beginnings of marriage to the post-parenting years. Mexican-American couples were different from others. In recalling the beginnings of marriage, seven out of ten Mexican Americans used words that conveyed highly positive memories compared to four out of ten whites and African Americans [X^2 (4, $N = 120$) = 10.00, $p = .04$]. The latter groups used more negative and ambivalent terms in describing communication patterns. Differences by ethnicity disappeared during the parenting years, primarily because of the deterioration in communication among Mexican-American couples which was linked to the sexual affairs of several husbands. After the children had grown to maturity, 92 percent of Mexican Americans spoke positively about marital communication compared to 54 percent of African Americans and 66 percent of whites [X^2 (4, $N = 120$) = 11.54, $p = .02$].

These findings may have reflected linguistic differences between the groups as well as the meanings associated with the term *communication*. Among African Americans and whites, communication was associated with ways in which individuals exchanged messages within relationships. Mexican Americans talked frequently about the totality of relationships, which included verbal but more importantly, general behavioral dimensions.

Communication over Time

The quality of communication changed throughout marriage. The longer people were married the better communication became. Prior to children, 44 percent of individuals remembered their communication as positive; by the third phase, after the youngest child was at least 18, 68 percent regarded their communication as positive.

Iris, a 72-year-old African-American woman married forty-eight years, commented on the change in her marriage:

He didn't always want to listen. Instead of discussing something, he'd get irritated because I didn't agree with him. But I think we do better now. As I said, at first, he wouldn't discuss anything, just leave. Rather than talk about it. So I'd have to persuade him that we needed to talk, we just had to talk. And I think as the years have gone by, I see that it's better. We can talk things out. . . . I think it's been a gradual process really . . . I think we finally found out how to talk . . . to watch others helped quite a lot. And I remember something that I haven't remembered for years. When he got mad, he would blow up, and he'd be yelling at me. And it wasn't that I had done something to him. Something had gone wrong and I was there. And I would have to remind him: "I'm on your side." And it finally got through. So we don't have that anymore. Communication, you have to keep on trying. . . . It's an ongoing thing.

Irwin, her 71-year-old spouse, described the process of change from his perspective:

She always tells me I never hear anything she has to say. She says: "You don't listen to me" . . . I guess there are times when I don't. I don't do it with the intent of being insulting or whatever. I guess just sometimes things come through, and they just keep right on going. . . . Early on, it probably did cause problems, but the longer we live together, the less I've done it. And I often hear a lot of things she doesn't think I hear.

The quality of communication varied by the phase of marriage. Several individuals, such as Jill, a 59-year-old professional woman married thirty-seven years, remembered the beginning of marriage as particularly difficult:

It is hard to remember because the first two years were not easy. They really were not easy because neither one of us knew about telling the other what we wanted. I was working and he was going to school. I had to work weekends. I would come home on a Sunday in the summer when it was hot. He wouldn't be home; he'd be at the beach. I would come home having worked really hard, you know, and he would be at the beach. So it took me a long time before I could say: "You know, I really want you home when I come home." I resented the fact that he was out at the beach. You know, things like that. It took a couple of years, and even then it wasn't great . . . we came from families that didn't talk, you know. And that was the way we were. . . . If we have a difference now, we get it out immediately.

Of the three phases of marriage, parenting confronted spouses with the most difficult challenges in communicating with each other. The teen-age years were especially difficult for many couples. In fact, we wonder whether the transition of adolescence does not confront many couples with a critical marital transition. While stressful for the marital relationship, it resulted in more open and mutually satisfying communication among many couples. Karen, a 51-year-old mother of four, described that period:

I think the hardest time that we had to communicate was when the kids were adolescents and teenagers ... I always thought Ken was a little too strict, and he always thought I was too lenient ... he would call me their lawyer ... the kids would say something, and Ken would say: "What! what!" and I'd say: "Oh well no, he didn't mean that ... " and Ken would say: "Let me see what your lawyer said ... that you really meant." That was a tense time too because we ended up sending all the kids to college, the finances ... actually, that phase when they started going off to college was starting to get to a better time, you know, then the years when you worried about them, when they are starting to drive cars. There were a lot of times that the kids told me things that they probably didn't tell Ken. And I had to decide if I should tell him or not. Sometimes I used to think that, you know, women are so different with kids ... I tell the kids how I feel, and listen to how they feel and I spent a lot of time communicating with the kids. I always thought that sometimes Ken will say what's important, but men don't do a lot of the small talk with the kids. He does a lot of it now, that the kids are older, not the small talk that mothers do. And I see it in a lot of families, and I think that, and I used to tell him, I used to say: "Ken, you know, try to talk more to them. He was always an excellent father; maybe I expected more because I come from a different background. My mother was like that, just talking all the time, communicating and that kind of thing. And as I said, that time was probably the hardest time for Ken and I, because it's stressful, you've got four kids that are in adolescence and they are all doing things, and they want to stay over at someones' house ... who's got the car ... that kind of thing. We never had any major trouble with them . . . that time was tough in communicating only because so much was happening ... that was a tough time. But as I said, nothing ever major, but just the raising of your children, those adolescent years.

For this blue-collar couple, adolescence had its socioeconomic stressors. Each spouse was committed to offering a college education to each of their four children who would be in college at the same time. As a consequence, Karen went to work and Ken worked overtime as much as he could to accomplish their goals. For many couples who were not as stressed by socioeconomic realities, the adolescent years were equally difficult for their relationships; their communication was also affected adversely.

Although communication improved , often dramatically, for many couples in the empty-nest years, the transition to being alone again created problems for some people. As Debra, a 62-year-old Jewish wife, observed, that period may have brought into relief a communication hole that was covered over throughout the marriage:

I don't think that I realized that there was a lack of communication and a lack of interests, common interests—until my children left the house and went to college. I don't know if I didn't realize it or if it just wasn't there. There was communication regarding a lot of things, but not regarding our relationship, not regarding feelings. It probably was lacking, but to be honest, I didn't realize it. And I don't have a sense that he did at all.

Communication about Conflict

We explored modes of communication between spouses when they were confronted with interpersonal conflicts. The most common way of communicating when individuals were not happy with their spouses was through withdrawal from relationships or withholding within relationships. Those methods were more characteristic of men than of women. Occasionally, withdrawal or withholding was described as a mutual defense. Harold and Heidi, an African-American couple who had been married thirty-seven years, described the symmetry in their defensive styles:

Harold described their communication as:

At times excellent. And then sometimes, not so good, and probably more on my part than hers ... lot of times I will keep things in. I catch myself not wanting to hurt her. But sometimes it does hurt her more by not knowing than letting her know. She'll notice and say: "Something's wrong. What's on your mind?" And she'll keep picking and badgering at me until I do finally sit down and talk. And she'll say: "Well, why didn't you say something from the beginning?"

The role of wives in breaking through impasses in communication was quite common. Heidi assumed that role while contending with her own mode of withdrawal:

There are times when we don't communicate and we do have problems.... It all depends on what the situation is. But see I can go sometimes almost two and three days and not say a word ... I hold something in for a while before I talk about it.

Occasionally, women would take dramatic action to communicate their unhappiness with men. From the perspective of a 67-year-old Jewish husband of forty-three years who had been preoccupied with other matters, the following memory was still vivid:

She looked forward to communicating and socializing and doing something and I'm downstairs hammering away at the nails. So that was part of the problem. But it had to be done. And I felt I had no choice. I didn't know, until sometime later, how much of a problem it was for her. And she brought it home to me ... I mention the wall with glass, because I was sitting in a chair just about like that—with the wall of glass behind me—and she threw a milk bottle at me. We had had a fight. One she probably wouldn't remember. She picked up a milk bottle and threw it. I think, in the forty some years we've been married, that is the absolutely worst single moment in the marriage ... I suddenly realized, which I obviously should have before that: "Hey, we've got a problem!" You know, that tends to shock you out of your mind.... And that was the end of the only really bad period in our marriage.

While arguments and verbal fights were common, one middle-class couple made a life-style out of bickering. They were unusual, however. More than communicating, fighting for them seemed to be a mode of connectedness, a way of being together and finding a mutually agreeable level of closeness. They had been married forty-one years, during which each had pursued highly successful careers. Irene reported:

We always bickered but did it all along while we were going together. I mean we bicker, but we're individuals and we have different ideas and opinions. We don't really have any serious fights about anything serious. It's stupid, picayune, dumb stuff most of the time. I'm stubborn and arrogant most of the time and he is easy going and we bicker.

Her husband, Ian:

We shouted a lot. Some people would probably say it was a constant argument, but it did not seem that way to us. We did not have big expectations.

The most common form of negotiating differences was through discussion and compromise. This Jewish couple who had been married twenty-six years described their mode of compromise. Henry acknowledged that

There was conflict, but I think we compromised. The only thing I can really sum up the relationship by is the word compromise ... if I had stayed on the track of being the authoritarian and she not accepting it, then we would have gone in two different directions. I think it's come to that whenever we've had conflict, there's always been compromise.

His wife, Hillary, commented on the strategy of compromise and the environments that were conducive to their working out disagreements:

> There's always sore spots, but you know, if you're going to talk to him about certain things, or he's going to talk to me about something, you don't want to do it at a certain time because ... there's going to be a little undercurrent. Our best time to talk is in the car or in a restaurant, I found, because you can't get angry in a restaurant and in a car you can't go anywhere. So if you do get angry, you have to stay there and work it out. That's our best times to talk.

Another mode of communication which several individuals reported was through writing to the spouse. Women did this more than men. Lilly, married thirty-eight years, described how she communicated to her spouse early in the marriage by putting her feelings into a letter:

> What I had to do in the beginning was I sat down and wrote him a letter. I would tell him how I felt about what was going on, whatever we were disagreeing about. Whether it was, like cleaning the house, it was always something dumb, never anything earth shattering. We did not disagree on any principle; it was just picky stuff. I would sit down and write him a letter. I did that two or three times, it worked fantastic. He would come home and say: "Gee, I didn't know you felt like that. I am sorry." It was better to put a little distance between us when trying to tell him my side; then he would think about it instead of flying off the handle.

Communication and Gender

Men and women frequently described different modes of communication within their marriages. Men appeared more uncomfortable than women in talking about their inner thoughts and feelings. Not infrequently, this led to tension in the relationship as these couples focused on their struggles to communicate about communication. For example, David, who had attained a leadership position that required superior negotiating skills, acknowledged that communication within his marriage was a source of tension:

> Even though I talked a lot, I'm a quiet person. I would say that one of the faults ... as I look back, is the communication, just being able to sit down and openly talk about anything. I do a lot of thinking, but it's sort of private thinking. We have our own conversations and we talked a lot. I would think that would be my biggest fault, that I'm not communicative enough ... but it's never been that if we start a conversation, I say, I don't want to talk about

it. We will always talk about anything that we felt was necessary to talk about. We could talk about anything. Communication ... would be a weak point in my relationship as far as coming in and talking about what I did all day. I don't want to go over it because sometimes it's been a bad day, sometimes it's been a good day but I'm not that communicative about my work. I don't bring it home, and maybe that's where the communication lack is. She knows what I do, but if you asked her to say what I did on my job she'd probably have two or three sentences on it ... also I probably have more empathy for money than I do for my kids but that's me.

Donna, his wife of thirty-six years and the mother of nine children, talked about the effect that David's inability in expressing his feelings had on her. She then described the lengthy process of adapting to a reality that had caused her considerable pain:

We don't talk a lot. I think a lot of the communication is done more just in deeds. David is not much of a person for expressing things, saying I look nice or compliments or things like that.... His way of showing me is by doing. He'll iron clothes, he'll do anything. When we first got married, I used to say you never say this or you never compliment me and he'd say "I show my love in what I do." I'm just not that way. There are times when I think: "How come he never compliments me anymore?" After a while, I realized. I would bring it up to him and ask him and he'd say because you know he's just not that way. He never has been and I don't think he ever will be. But I know he loves me by what he does . . . I'm a person who always loved to be complimented, and I liked to be told that I look nice. It isn't that he never did, but it's not a lot. Now, I don't need it as much as I did when I was younger anyway. But it would have been nice to have him say things like that more often than he did.

With other couples, communication differences between males and females were present in the marriage, yet did not appear to have the same effect on relationships as they did with David and Donna. For these people, marriage was experienced as a type of oasis where spouses could talk in an intimate manner. Kiko and Krystal, a Mexican-American couple married twenty-four years, spoke to that theme:

KIKO: The communication between us is the most important thing and that's why we're still together ... I'm the kind of person who doesn't like to share my feelings with anybody and Krystal, obviously she knows things. I share with her my very deepest feelings, so the communication between me and her was always good. Some way or another we always find the time to talk about our problems between each other.

KRYSTAL: Well, it's one of the things that I think make it work. We talk to each other. I bore people to death. I like talking and that's one thing I told him. If you have a problem, if you don't like something, tell me. There's no way I can know, if you don't let me know. I might be thinking that everything is so perfect and everything is so smooth and it's not because you don't want to tell me. We discuss. We argue.... He has a real quick temper and he doesn't know how to talk and make people understand his point without getting agitated. But not with me.

Communication and Early Socialization

In the overview of communication, in the initial stage of marriage, differences between Mexican-American couples and others were discussed. Here, we focus on qualitative differences between spouses based on variations in their backgrounds. Some individuals associated their ethnic backgrounds with difficulties in communicating within marriage. For them, the marital relationship became a means for modifying ingrained styles of encoding and decoding messages. Ivan and Irene, who had been married twenty-six years, talked about that dynamic. Ivan reflected on his background and his mode of communicating with Irene:

I have a tendency to play the cards very close to the vest, and I, at that time, more so than now, kept my own counsel.... Again it's probably the role model that was cast for you from early childhood that you were expected to be the bread winner, take on the burdens, and whatever pressures you were suppose to suffer them in silence. The Irish Catholic upbringing where you certainly didn't cry in your beer. It wasn't acceptable ... I guess it was my lack of having a warm and charming personality and being very close mouthed, and it bothered the hell out of her. There were certainly occasions when you'd try to punish each other, be moody, sulky, not communicative. We certainly had different periods of that existence.... One thing that was early on was that you never fess up to anything. So that I never fessed up to anything.

As counterpoint to her husband, Irene related the following:

Overall, I would say it's probably pretty good and effective communication. When it comes to that personal feeling level, neither one of us really ever, ever, learned too much about what it's like to let the other person know what you're feeling and what your needs are. And him too, I'm sure. He stifled and stuffed a lot. And I'm sure that there's a lot of things about me that I do that he would change but he's never said anything about it, so I have no way of knowing what makes him unhappy or what he'd like to do different. Because he doesn't tell me so ... I think we've grown. I do think that we have grown. I think that we both probably still would think twice about what we were going to say. I guess that would be a good way to put it; I don't think either one of us is that spontaneous. I think we both probably think too much ... a little spontaneity would be a big improvement.

Understanding the influence of family background and respect for individual modes of defending against unsettling feelings were important factors in the development of positive communication. Fred and Fran, both in their early sixties and married for forty years, spoke of how these factors nurtured a balance of closeness and distance in their relationship. Fred recalled:

In the beginning, communicating was tough ... I used to say to myself, well, she's not Italian. And she doesn't know my moods as an Italian. I grew up with ten brothers and sisters and a mother and father, in a very stable home with big meals and friends and relatives and open house and that type of thing. And then you look back at her house ... it was cold. It was a mother and father who drank. It was a mother and a kid sister. It was not knowing what she's going to find when she comes home. So, I used to try to take that into consideration. I think it's caring for the person more than anything else. ... We know each other's anger now. We've never been physical. But I know by the tone of her voice when it's time to stop and she knows by the tone of my voice when enough is enough ... that's the point when we walk away ... because I respect her feelings about being angry and there's no sense in pursuing it because it's just gonna get worse, so either I walk away or she walks away.

For Fran, respect and determination to let her husband know how she felt were central to the viability of their relationship:

I think respect is a very important thing because when you get pushy and that sort of thing, then that's not good and there's a lot of misunderstanding because you don't talk. You've got to talk. You've got to talk. You've got to tell the person, even though you're afraid it's gonna hurt their feelings, you've just got to let him know.

The observations of these two couples conveyed the critical role that individual backgrounds had in shaping marital communication. Ethnicity along with other family dynamics was of particular importance. The personal histories of individuals, which had become a part of them, had a powerful effect on how each couple negotiated the balance of closeness to distance in their relationship.

SUMMARY

Mirroring the prevailing cultural mores of the post–World War II era when these individuals married, their expectations of self and spouse were differentiated along gender lines. Women expected to stay at home, become mothers, and care for their families. Men expected to work outside of the home so as to provide for their families. That differentiation of gender roles began to change after marriage as couples were confronted with the realities of family life. While men continued to be primarily instrumental in their orientations to marital roles, women integrated both instrumental and expressive orientations. The differentiation by gender was reflected in how spouses talked of fitting together. Rather than a symmetrical fit in which individuals experience self and other as more rather than less equal relational partners, these relationships were characterized by complementarity. That is, individual differences characterized how spouses fit together in relationships. No doubt, that was reinforced by societal values about the acceptable roles of men and women in marriage.

Throughout these marriages, specific qualities were identified which clarified how husbands and wives related to each other. The perceptions of spouse sensitivity and understanding were different. From the beginning of their relationships to the empty-nest phase, husbands perceived wives as more sensitive and understanding compared to themselves; wives perceived husbands as less sensitive and understanding than they were. Although men felt that relationships were equitable during the parenting phase, women remembered feeling that the relationships were not fair for them.

Communication patterns were variable depending on ethnicity. Although communication deteriorated among Mexican Americans during the parenting years, it improved slightly for whites and African Americans. The deterioration in Mexican-American marriages was associated with the sexual affairs of husbands. Even with these variations, the quality of communication changed the longer one was married. During the empty-nest years, most husbands and wives reported less serious conflict and more openness in their relationships.

REFERENCES

Barnes, M. L. & Buss, D. M. (1985). Sex differences in the interpersonal behavior of married couples. *Journal of Personality and Social Psychology, 48,* 654–661.

Billings, A. (1979). Conflict resolution in distressed and nondistressed married couples. *Journal of Consulting and Clinical Psychology, 47,* 368–376.

Chelune, G. J., Rosenfeld, L. B., & Waring, E. M. (1985). Spouse disclosure patterns in distressed and nondistressed couples. *The American Journal of Family Therapy, 13* (4), 24–32.

Chodorow, N. (1978). *The reproduction of mothering: Psychoanalysis and the sociology of gender.* Berkeley: University of California Press.

Gilligan, C. (1982). *In a different voice: Psychological theory and women's development.* Cambridge, MA: Harvard University Press.

Gottman, J. M. (1982). Emotional responsiveness in marital conversation. *Journal of Communication, 32,* 108–120.

Lewis, R. A. & Spanier, G. B. (1979). Theorizing about the quality and stability of marriage. In W. Burr, L. Nye, R. Hill, & I. Reiss (Eds.), *Contemporary Theories about the Family* (pp. 268–294). Glencoe, IL: The Free Press,

Mason, K. O. & Bumpass, L. L. (1975). U.S. women's sex-role ideology, 1970. *American Journal of Sociology, 80,* 1212–1219.

Noller, P. (1984). *Nonverbal communication and marital interaction.* Oxford, England: Pergamon Press.

Rosenfeld, L. B., & Welsh, S. M. (1985). Differences in self-disclosure in dual-career and single-career marriages. *Communication Monographs, 52,* 253–263.

Surrey, J. L. (1984). Self-in-relation: A theory of women's development. *Work in Progress, No. 13.* Wellesley, MA: Stone Center Working Paper Series.

Watzlawick, P., Beavin, J., & Jackson, D. (1967). *Pragmatics of human communication: A study of interactional patterns, pathologies and paradoxes.* New York: W. W. Norton & Company.

White, K. M., Speisman, J. C., Jackson, D., Bartis, S., & Costos, D. (1986). Intimacy maturity and its correlates in young married couples. *Journal of Personality and Social Psychology, 50,* 152–162.

—3—

Conflict

she preferred to discuss and talk it out but that's just not my shtick . . .
it's a trait I have . . .

As in any primary relationships that endure, conflicts were inevitable in
these marriages. States of interpersonal disharmony were manifested in
several forms during the early years, throughout parenting, and into the
post-parenting years. Rarely did conflicts have a neutral effect on the
well-being of spouses and the future of their marriages. Although they
occasionally led to deterioration in relationships, conflicts usually resulted
in adaptive changes. Developmentally, these couples moved through conflictual periods which created opportunities for personal and marital growth
(Demment,1992; Hamel, 1993; Kanter, 1993; Mengden, 1994; Podbelski,1993) that was contingent on the capacity and readiness of both spouses
to change (Nadelson, Polonski, & Matthews, 1984).

It is important to clarify that we were trying to understand conflicts from
the perspectives of individual spouses—that is, from the inside out rather
than from the outside in. In reviewing interview transcripts, the points of
view of respondents have been respected, and judgments were made on the

basis of what reality meant to each of them. A team approach, which included double-blind coding of conflict themes, helped to neutralize subjectivity and professional opinions.

The challenge was not to decide whether conflicts existed but to assess their severity. Distinctions were made between minimal and major conflicts on the basis of how respondents perceived problems, tensions, and differences. If people described a conflict as highly distressing to them personally and as having significant disruptive effects on their marital relationships, the conflict was considered major. Relatively few individuals talked of major conflicts; most conflicts described by respondents were coded as being minimal.

Husbands and wives were remarkably consistent in describing the kinds and severity of conflicts throughout the three phases of marriage. Twelve percent of the spouses recalled major conflicts early in their marriages, a figure that rose to 29 percent during child-rearing and then fell to 7 percent in the empty-nest years. These patterns did not vary significantly by gender, ethnicity, or education.

In this chapter, the nature of marital conflicts is explored, as well as the ways in which spouses coped with differences between them. Because of the economic and ethnic diversity of the sample, there was an opportunity to explore how two social stressors, lack of money and racism, affected marriages, especially among blue-collar white, African-American, and Mexican-American couples. Sixty-five percent of respondents had less than a college education. That group, defined operationally as "blue collar," was evenly divided among white, African-American, and Mexican-American respondents. Fifteen percent of whites had current family incomes under $50,000 compared to 71 percent of African Americans and 92 percent of Mexican Americans. We wondered whether the stresses associated with lack of money and racism exacerbated marital conflict. The discussion then focuses on conflicts in the early years, during child-rearing, and into the empty-nest period. The last half of the chapter identifies the methods through which spouses handled interpersonal conflicts.

ECONOMIC STRESS

The lack of money was a significant stressor for several marriages. Forty-seven percent of white respondents, 61 percent of African Americans, and 67 percent of Mexican Americans reported finances as having negative effects in the early years of marriage [X^2 (4, $N = 120$) = 16.12, $p = .003$]. The effects of family incomes became less stressful during the empty-nest years for whites (16 percent) and African Americans (46 percent). However, income continued to be a stressor for 75 percent of Mexican Americans [X^2 $(4, N = 120) = 44.61, p = < .001$].

Despite the stressful effects of low incomes on blue-collar marriages, money did not lead to major conflicts. As people talked about the lack of money, the theme of interpersonal strain became apparent. Fred, a white construction worker with five children, recalled:

> When we were first married, seven out of every ten discussions or arguments we had were about money. . . I think the insecurity of work, being in construction and the finances not being secured were a main source of disagreement. So I think it was financial worry . . . a sense of my feeling I wasn't able to provide, and she could not handle the finances of the house and all that went with it. I think that . . . can kill friendship or a love affair pretty quick.

Although financial circumstances improved for white couples, that was not true for most minority couples. For them, low incomes and poverty were a chronic source of strain. Ignacio, a 51-year-old Mexican-American father of five children, described how a marginal family income impacted his marriage:

> I give her . . . all the money and let her do whatever she wants to do with it, bills or whatever. She's the one that pays the bills, has the money in the bank and knows how much we have and makes the checks out . . . if I did, I'd probably go haywire and make checks out all over. If I see something I want, I'll buy it . . . she tells me, you can't have no money in your pocket, because you'll just spend it, which is true. When she'll get behind on payments, I know that it's nobody's fault but ours. We don't make a lot of money, but she'll want something for the kids or the house and she'll think ahead: "Well I'm supposed to get so much money next week, so I'll go ahead and spend what I have here." Then next week comes, or something else happens and that money is not there. I keep telling her: "You can't think that way; you've got to do with what you have and don't plan on what you don't have." I blame her and I know it's both of our faults. I blame her because she's the one that takes care of it . . . it's been like this for twenty-nine years.

In order to cope with the stresses associated with low incomes, since blue-collar men were also subjected to periodic unemployment, women frequently became employed. Occasionally, this created new problems in relationships. An African-American couple in their fifties spoke to that conflict and how they coped with it. Justin said:

Basically, the only problem we have now is with financing . . . trying to make ends meet. Things have changed around because I was out of work for a long while, and then we got behind on a lot of things. So it's making things tough. We have a few little squabbles over that. But it's nothing that really makes things that bad. But it just is doing a few things to us that we haven't been through in a lot of years. But luckily, we do know how to cope with it, and we sit down and talk it over . . . we might have a little yelling match or something like that. But at least we'll sit down and we'll apologize to each other and it's over with.

His wife, Jane, described how the power balance in their relationship changed as a result of his unemployment and her getting a job:

When he used to tell me I couldn't do this and I couldn't do that, we used to get into big fights, really. Because I wasn't working, I was just taking care of the house and everything. But when I started working, and making money, that's when we would have the little conflict, because he would say: "You can't do it." And I would say: "I can do it because I have my own money." So that's when we ran into conflict. So naturally, you're going to run into it, because you're working eight hours, and whatever, and you have your own money, you're more independent.

For several couples, the stress of low incomes brought them closer together and strengthened their commitment to the marriage. A Mexican-American woman commented on how she responded to that type of stress:

Instead of a strain I think you get closer. Because I know that the biggest burden he worries about is financial security . . . instead of a strain, I think we got closer because I would try to make things more comfortable, try to soften that blow of that financial strain.

Religion, particularly among minority couples, played an important role in coping with economic stresses. As we shall see, religion was also very important in coping with racism. Cenci, a 63-year-old Mexican American married for forty years, described the importance of religious beliefs:

The hardest thing for me was to be on a strict budget, especially when I had my children, because they came one after the other . . . it was hard for me. I wasn't working and that extra income didn't come in. It was hard for me to be on a strict budget. But I never told him that I wished I wouldn't have married, like a lot of people do. I never said anything like that at all. I knew God would help out. I knew that the Holy Spirit gave me strength and I was the churchgoer while my husband was not. He never would go to church . . .

after we married, he would go, but at first he wouldn't go. I think that really helped me to have my Lord on my side and the Holy Spirit. I knew he would give me strength . . . I've always had religion in my life, and I think that helped me a lot.

If religion offered people solace and comfort, hope held out a future that would be better than the one they had known. A 74-year-old African American, Kirk, offered this poignant memory:

We figured that in time . . . jobs would come. We would take these walks into town and see washing machines in the window, and we would say: "Some day we're going to have a washing machine." When we first got married, we had an icebox; you had to put the ice in the top, and a pan underneath where the water dripped in. And we had an oil stove and I had to carry the oil upstairs. My wife made diapers and changed them and washed them and used them the next time. We didn't have a shower; I thought to live in an apartment with a shower would be about the end of the world. We had . . . no television; we didn't even have a record player. We had our dreams in the movies. We used to go to the movies and see things . . . I didn't say it too often, but I would say: "Someday we're going to be like that." And gradually things did fall into place.

These couples experienced the anxiety and the consequences that resulted from limited financial resources. More often than not, spouses worked together in order to cope with financial strain, and their relationships grew stronger.

The financial problems of couples from higher socioeconomic levels were expressed in different ways. Conflicts about money generally suggested struggles with power and control as well as clashes in personalities. A 45-year-old successful businessman, Kent, married for twenty-three years with two children, observed:

It's funny how you forget the bad things, or you try to. I have a knack of knocking things out of my mind or suppressing them, but there was a period we were always going at it . . . and if I remember, money was involved. There was always the lack of enough to do everything we wanted to do. And I've always been blamed; she's always accused me, when she wasn't working, of not giving her enough money to enjoy herself and to do the shopping and stuff. What I am is . . . I'm conservative and I like to make sure—I've always done the books. She has never taken charge of the money in the house, so I'm always watching where everything's going and every penny is going.

His 44-year-old wife Kim, agreed that finances were a major problem:

Probably the money thing.... That's the thing we've fought about the most.

Her husband brought similar traits of control which made him successful in business into his marital relationship. In the relationship, he supervised and restricted Kim's freedom to make decisions about how to spend money for personal and household expenses. As the marriage developed, she became frustrated and angry. His controlling and withholding style diminished the closeness in their relationship and led to repeated conflicts about power and control issues.

RACISM

Although minority respondents talked extensively of the effects of racism on their lives, few reported any significant consequences of racism on marital relationships. Unlike Mexican Americans who did not think they were the objects of racism, African Americans often described their experiences with eloquence and poignancy. Perhaps the differences between these two minority groups were related to their social circumstances. Mexican Americans were reared and continued to live in close-knit communities that offered considerable protection from a world that was potentially as oppressive to them as it was to African Americans. As we have pointed out, the African Americans had migrated from other parts of the country, usually the South, and were cut off from the support and protection of their extended families. Also, the geographic regions in which these two groups resided were different. Most African Americans lived in northeastern metropolitan areas in which they were a minority. Mexican Americans lived in smaller southwestern communities in which they were a majority. As respondents expressed themselves, Mexican Americans focused on the oppressive effects of poverty and African Americans on racism.

African Americans talked of how they had coped with and survived racism. Amy, a 65-year-old woman, talked of resiliency, a theme evident in the lives of many individuals:

I try to find a reason why people act the way they do. I've ... been hurt so deeply. But I always had this ability, and I think this is very true in the black race. . . . People get hurt very deeply but they have the ability to pick themselves up and go on. They have a resilience about them. I never held a grudge or anything. I'll get mad, explode, stuff like that. But it's not anything that knocks you out, no. You just say: "Hey, that's another thing that happened." And you get up and keep going. You learn to shut it off ... by just not letting it get to you.... If you did, you wouldn't exist. I had a lot of real bad, bad emotional blows that I've had to deal with ... especially with my children, trying to help them realize that life is bigger than some little things that happen: when people called them names, not being invited to birthday parties, not being included in a game or something like that. And so I had to deal with a lot with my children growing up. And I think I helped most of them. But that was a challenge for me back in the 70s when they were teenagers. I wanted them to grow up and realize that there was something better waiting.

Among African-American men, coping with racism was often a matter of confronting it or trying to ignore it. It was common for men to ignore racist remarks as a way of surviving in the world. In the response of George, 63 years old, one can feel the underlying rage contained in his pain:

I'd hear people holler at me and say things, but it really didn't upset me that bad.... I didn't care. As long as a person didn't put their hand on me, I didn't care what they said really. And I still feel that way today. If somebody wants to call you names, forget about it. So I always try to live a certain way, a decent way of life, the best I know, and I really don't worry about the things people say. At work and other places, I almost completely ignore it. I don't let people rattle my cage ... I just go on. I'm a funny person.... I just don't let it bother me, although I know it's there ... but I don't go looking for it.

Occasionally, some men were confrontational in dealing with the white world which had made them the objects of insensitive remarks. Irwin described how African-American men sometimes dealt with racism:

Sometimes when I had some flack from people, I threw it back at them.... There's other times I ignore them. Like the guy I've known for years ... we were talking about people's backgrounds: Irish, English, German, whatever. And he says: "Jeez, what the hell are you?" I said: "What do you mean, what am I? My great grandmother was born here; she was a slave. My grandmother was born here. My mother was born here. My father was born here. And I was born here. So what the hell am I? I'm a black American!"

Religious beliefs were a valuable resource for several African Americans, helping them cope with the assaultiveness of racism on their self-respect. Bob, 71 years old, talked of how religion enabled him to endure by checking the expression of his rage and reframing the problem:

I've been called all kinds of names. And if it hadn't been for my religion I wouldn't be here. I would have busted them in the mouth. But I just, you know, let it go and say: "You don't know any better," you know, and let it go at that. Like my wife said, I've got patience like Job. A lot of times I'd take it and she wouldn't. She's quick like that, you know, but me, I'm not. I just laugh and tell 'em: "You don't know any better." You just let it roll off.

Though infrequently, respondents did talk about how the marriage was a refuge in dealing with racism. Spouses found support in one another which was identified by a 64-year-old husband, Art:

It probably made it stronger. I'd come home from a particularly tiring day and if something like that had happened we'd discuss it. Certainly we supported each other in that. And it made our relationship stronger because when you support each other . . . you seem to grow stronger, I believe.

Sometimes, the complementary nature of spouses' temperaments served as a valuable resource. One husband commented on his wife's calmness which balanced his temper. He was referring to their reactions to racial incidents:

I was always hoping she was with me, because she would always calm me down and keep me from doing something foolish.

Heidi saw the matter somewhat differently:

Actually, Harold ran into it more than I really have. But he brings it home and talks about it. But he generally will say what he has to say before he even tells me about it.

Two themes emerged from the observations of African-American women as they talked about racism and their marriages. One theme addressed the role of wives in offering husbands unconditional support. Some women referred to their responsibility for developing and maintaining their homes as a special place for African-American men, a supportive oasis from the outside world. Beth spoke to that theme:

The only thing we had was ourselves. . . . what keeps black people together, as much as they are, are families. I don't know if whites ever realize that. . . . This is why I can't make Bob feel uncomfortable inside these doors. He has enough adversity outside. When he comes in here he's king of the mountain. I do whatever it takes to make him feel like somebody. The world gives him, as a black male, enough hassle. He doesn't need a hassle at home. And this is what I try to teach young black women. Never hassle your husband at home. He's got the world on his shoulders, dragging his ass around. And sometimes he's going to come home upset, not with you, but he's upset with the world out there and the deal he got today, another turndown that he got on his job. He's gonna need that drink. He's going to need that extra helping of supper. And he's going to get a little fat maybe. He's going to do a lot of things he wouldn't do normally. Maybe he'll need an extra dose of sex. Who knows. Maybe he ain't gonna have no sex at all. But remember that he's in a cruel hostile world. He takes more than a man's share. And I would never want anybody to put my husband down as a man, say he's not a man ... You know. They live on the edge all the time. You worry about it, you have dreams, nightmares about your men. It's not easy ... when you know they're struggling and doing their best for their abilities.

For African-American women, respect grew as they understood the struggles of black men, including their husbands, to survive in a world that was often demeaning of them. Carol, a 51-year-old woman, reflected on this second theme. In responding to a question about how racism may have affected her marriage, she said:

I never thought of it in that way ... we had to deal with people in order to keep some semblance of self-respect and not be walked over and yet still not be killed ... I was oblivious to a lot of things. I didn't think in the black and white mode. I just thought this is my family. ... But when I think back now, I think, boy, I don't know how I did that ... I just worked to try and improve things for us and for those who came after us ... I've learned a lot along those lines ... I never realized how much black males have had to deal with on an overall basis. I mean you read statistics and you read this and that, but until you actually see the system in motion you wonder why sometimes more black males haven't committed suicide or whatever ... just the negativeness of circumstances in which they're placed. No matter what their qualifications are, they never seem to be able to move ahead in a timely fashion.

To summarize, although low income was a source of considerable stress for blue-collar couples early in marriage, that factor did not generate major, disruptive conflicts in these marriages. On the contrary, social stressors sometimes strengthened the bonds between husbands and wives. Poverty among Mexican Americans and racism among African Americans may have reinforced a need to work together in order to survive and to contend with the threats of the external world.

THE EARLY YEARS: ROLE TRANSITIONS

Compared to 20 percent of Protestants and 14 percent of Catholics, no Jewish respondents reported major conflicts early in marriage [X^2 (2, $N =$ 120) = 6.45, p =.04]. That finding was likely related to the ascription of marital roles among Jews, which had a neutralizing effect on potential conflict as spouses negotiated transitions into early marital relationships (Levinson, 1986). More than any other conflict, Jewish respondents focused on in-laws; mothers of husbands were identified as a "problem" in three out of ten of their marriages. Usually, the issues involved separation from the mother and commitment to the wife. Brian talked about the dilemma of dealing with his mother and wife:

It was when my mother was alive. And Bernice would literally, not figuratively, literally, get terrible headaches when we had to go see her. We would see her on special days. Not very often, but the holidays were requirements. Bernice would get migraine headaches when we had to go over there. I think she felt that I should have been much more firm with my mother and put her down and not accepted her attitude as I did. My attitude was, What is that going to gain me? Let's go over there. Spend two necessary hours and then get the hell out. Bernice felt that I should have been much more firm with my mother. Not let her get away with whatever it was she was getting away with. I think, we had a difference of opinion there. I think, in retrospect, I probably wouldn't do it any differently. Because I still feel that I wouldn't have gained anything. At one point I did get angry with my mother and she left the house in a huff, crying. It didn't get us anywhere. It didn't change anything. It didn't do any good. That may be the meek way out. I just thought it was the logical way out.

Bernice described the conflicts in the following way:

His parents liked me a lot when I was his sister's girlfriend, but as soon as I was Brian's girlfriend, they didn't like me anymore and we had a lifetime of hell because of that. All through our marriage she never accepted me as a real daughter-in-law. She had three daughters. What'd she need another one for? And I took her son away. This was very unique, I thought, to someone born in this country, to have an attitude like that.

Although these intergenerational conflicts were serious and caused unhappiness throughout their marriage, Brian and Bernice did not consider them to be major conflicts. Perhaps his denial and her displacement of feelings helped to contain the conflict so that it did not appear to have a major effect on their marriage.

Among Protestants and Catholics, conflicts were identified in negotiating marital roles, which usually involved a clash between expectations and reality. Family backgrounds and differences in personality resulted in conflict similar to that recalled by Grover, a 53-year-old engineer:

> When we first got married, my expectations of marriage was what I learned in the household ... certainly that changed almost right off the bat. In the first few years it changed because I realized the marriage did not have to be like my parents' marriage.... My expectations changed within the first three to five years. Completely got away from holding my parents' marriage as an expectation as to what ours should be. Since then, I don't think it really changed that much.

His spouse, Gladys, reflected on the reciprocal changes in their relationship which began in the first year of marriage. From her perspective, the process of change continued for many years after that:

> When we had an argument I would quickly yell: "Let's get divorced." Finally, Grover said to me: "If you really mean it, say it, if you don't, then don't say it!" We have been married thirty-one years, and I have not uttered those words again. I did not realize how I was hurting him. I was immature then and did not think of it in those terms. He spelled it out. As we got older, the funny things were that Grover became the risk taker and I became less the risk taker. We switched roles.

THE CHILD-REARING YEARS: PARENTING CONFLICTS AND DISAFFECTION

During the parenting years, 30 percent of the respondents described major conflicts in their marriages. These conflicts revolved around two interrelated themes: lack of emotional relatedness between spouses and the rearing of children, especially adolescents. Although the deterioration in relatedness was not always connected to being parents, children made demands on parents which compromised the exclusiveness of marital relationships which had characterized the early years of marriage. In becoming mothers, women needed to invest emotionally in their children. Some men, such as this middle-aged father of three, felt a loss as they had to share their wives with children:

When the kids come along, they have a way of bursting the bubble and making things less than perfect.

Several respondents had similar reactions to the stress parenthood placed on their marriages. Bernice, a high school graduate and homemaker with two children, expressed feelings of being overwhelmed by the pressures of rearing a family:

The beginning and the end are the same. The middle was awful in my life. I don't think I would've had children. I wish I didn't have children. I wasn't ready for them.

Her husband, Brian, had a similar observation:

I'll tell you one thing that made life better—was when the kids left us.... The kids, more than any single thing in our life, I think are the cause of many of the problems. They have problems. They're expensive. Sometimes they don't live up to your expectations, although they are living up to their own. And they deny you a great deal of freedom.

When couples were slow to recognize and negotiate complementary shifts in their relationships required by the needs of children, conflicts resulted and marital satisfaction lessened. The rearing of children required change that was difficult for several couples to manage. There was less time for marital intimacy; women experienced less autonomy and increased stress as primary caretakers. During this period, spouses talked of a decline in feelings of relatedness; women more than men reported less fairness in the marriages.

Of all the subphases of child-rearing, adolescence was the most stressful for couples. Comments about difficulties in the rearing of children during the adolescent years were consistent among many respondents; conflicts related to enforcing discipline and setting limits were plentiful. Faith, a college graduate, had painful memories of her relationship with her adolescent daughter:

The most difficult times were our daughter's teen years. The relationship between the three of us was difficult. We had screaming fights. She asserted her individuality and thought we knew nothing.

A second dimension of conflict in the child-rearing years was the estrangement between spouses and what was expressed as a decline in feelings of relatedness compared to the early years. Kayser (1993) has referred to this state as marital disaffection. In contrast to her findings, disaffection among the couples in this study was a time-limited state that disappeared once the children were grown. Almost one-third of the respondents talked of a decline in relatedness, which resulted in sexual affairs among a few husbands. No wives talked of having affairs. A father of four children described the process which included infidelity, talk of divorce, and eventual rapprochement:

> I think the worst was after we started having the children, because in my opinion I kind of took it for granted. When you have a woman you more or less take advantage of her because if you know a woman is going to be good and faithful to you, you're going to go out and do the opposite thing, and that's what happened to me. We've had our rough times. We've been on the verge of trying to get a divorce ... but it didn't go through because I told her I was going to shape up my life, because back then I was still going out ... we managed to sort things out and the kids started growing up.

As children entered young adulthood and parents were alone again, couples were positive about the transition into a new marital structure; an increase in relatedness and satisfaction with marriage was reported.

THE EMPTY-NEST YEARS

Few respondents described any major conflicts with their marriages after the children were grown. Most were able to negotiate the transition of being alone again and to enjoy the freedom from the responsibilities of child-rearing. For several spouses, the post-parenting years took on the qualities of a rapprochement in their love which had been compromised during the preceding phase. Only eight individuals (7 percent) talked of major conflicts in the post-parenting years; these conflicts were usually derivatives of earlier difficulties. Women were more likely than men to describe major conflicts which reflected that theme.

Irene, married for twenty-six years with three children, recounted a long struggle with a lack of emotional relatedness. She went into counseling for a brief period because she felt unhappy and thought there had to be a more fulfilling way to have her needs met:

> I've taken a look, and decided that until I get rid of the dissatisfaction with my own feelings that nothing else is going to change. But I guess that the lack of involvement is what I would have to say was underlying my feeling of

dissatisfaction ... he's home every day, he works all the time, he doesn't beat me, he doesn't drink, he doesn't run around, what is my problem? There's no major thing ... but there is a lot more to relationships than those external things. I just didn't have that self-confidence to rock the boat ... and I never felt sure enough of myself that our relationship could sustain conflict or believe enough that what I wanted to do was important. Somehow or another I always believed that what he was doing was more important. The stuff that I was doing wasn't going to make much difference. Which is pretty sad.

In thinking further about her unhappiness, she continued:

Every time closeness became an issue, you go clean up your act for a while and you try a little harder and you make a stronger commitment and that carries you for a year or two until you have another dealing with the fact that I've had enough of this crap and here we are back in the same spot. There were a couple of times when we seriously considered getting a separation ... maybe there was something in my life that I missed because I married so young. Maybe you'd be better off, you know, separating. He always couldn't understand what my problem was, what my discontent was. Everything is fine. But things are not fine.

Ivan had this comment about what Irene described as disaffection in their marriage:

There was some tense couple of years before we recognized that there had to be some action taken and we went through the counseling period. I think we've become fairly content with each other. You have a sense that you are not going to bend somebody to your will or shape ... I would like to think that she has accepted me. She certainly has probably changed me some, but I don't see myself as being significantly different.

Although Irene acknowledged her chronic unhappiness, she did not have the confidence to leave the relationship:

At this point in your life it gets to the point where it kinda gets scary to think about starting your life all over again. Am I that unhappy? Will I be any happier in another situation? I just ask myself all those questions, and I don't know whether I've made the decision to settle for less or just accept the fact that it's not gonna change, and I can live with it the way it is. One of the primary things is that I don't feel that he loves me, I know that he does. And I know that he'd do anything I ask him to do except enjoy life ... you know, share ... I guess ... being alone looked a lot less comfortable.

Ivan and Irene were an unusual couple in this study because they had chronic unresolved conflicts. For most couples, there was an increase in intimacy, sharing, support, and satisfaction once the children matured. Harold, an African American, who at 56 had been married for thirty-seven years with five children, captured that theme:

> Well, I feel if it wasn't for this relationship, I don't know where I would be today. I think it was one of the best things that ever happened to me ... she influences my life a lot. And I'm just as much in love with her today as I was thirty-seven years ago.

HANDLING CONFLICTS

Because respondents were interviewed separately, we were able to assess how each spouse experienced not only their own but also their spouse's style of dealing with conflict. The data led us to conceptualize a continuum of predominant modes of behavior with avoidance at one pole and confrontation at the other. Avoidance included any defensive maneuvers to deny or to escape face-to-face discussion of differences. Confrontation included any effort to express one's thoughts and feelings directly to the spouse in a face-to-face encounter.

In the beginning phase of marriage and extending into the parenting years, several women expressed considerable conflict about their husband's lack of availability and unwillingness to talk with them about differences. Men had little resistance in discussing their behaviors with us, acknowledging their avoidant patterns, observing how different they were from their spouses, and pointing out how they had changed. What surprised us were the similarities between the observations of wives and husbands about their own and their spouses' modes of handling differences and dealing with interpersonal conflict. That finding has importance for the validity of the data. It also may have considerable relevance for understanding why these marriages survived for more than thirty years.

Findings about the ways in which interpersonal differences and conflict were handled, particularly by males in the early years of marriage, were compatible with those in other studies (Komarovsky, 1962; Rubin, 1976). For example, Lewis (1988) found that women were "relationship specialists" who were responsible for communication in marriage; as a consequence, they took the initiative in problem solving. According to Lewis, men were more likely to avoid conflict. Although current evidence suggests that these gender differences persist throughout life (McGee & Wells, 1982;

O'Neil, Fishman & Kinsella-Shaw, 1987; Zube, 1982), men may become less instrumental and more expressive as they grow older (Hyde & Phillis, 1979), as was seen among several men in our study. Concurrently, women may seek personal fulfillment outside of the home through work and other activities (Zube, 1982). This tendency was common among middle-class women in our study. Less affluent women were employed outside the home in order to help with household expenses and to pay for the college tuitions of their children.

Avoidance to Confrontation

Throughout marriage, gender was central in shaping modes of handling conflict. Most men were avoidant and most women confrontational. Sixty-eight percent of the men described themselves as avoidant during the early years of marriage; during the same period, 62 percent of the women described themselves as confrontational [X^2 (1, $N = 120$) = 10.85, $p =$ < .001]. Bill and Brenda, both college graduates who had been married twenty-nine years, spoke to that theme.

> BILL: I think Brenda preferred to discuss and talk it out, but that's just not my shtick and I know that and it's not a particularly admirable trait, but it's a trait I have ... she would rather face it head on.

> BRENDA: We have very different styles. Yes. I'm quick to anger, but then I forget and say: "OK, I'm done." He's the opposite.

Among a few couples, complementarity in handling differences was reversed. Homero, a Mexican American, speaks of the beginning of his marriage to Herminia thirty years ago:

> We might have been married about a year; we had a disagreement over something, and like the people you see in movies, she got upset and walked off. She went to bed and about a half an hour later I went in there and she said, No you're not going to sleep in here ... that was the last straw. I turned all the lights on and said that she needed to get up out of bed so that we can talk about this. She said she didn't want to, but I said we are going to talk about it because you need to understand one thing: "That will never happen in my house. If it ever gets to the point that you and I can't talk about something, come to an agreement or compromise or something. If it gets to the point where we can't talk, I'll just get my things and I'm out the door. It's as simple as that, so stop and think about it before we stop talking to each

other." . . . Really, when we stop and think about it, our arguments are over stupid things. Nothing could be that important.

Cultural Variations

In addition to gender, the other independent variables that yielded significant differences were religion and ethnicity. Mutual confrontation was a method of handling differences among 64 percent of African Americans in the beginning of marriage; the comparable rate for whites and Mexican Americans was 40 percent [X^2 (2, $N = 120$) = 6.62, $p = .04$]. Art, a 64-year-old African-American male married for forty-five years, described mutual confrontation in the following way:

> We have done a lot of screaming at each other, and pouting if you will and storming off and screaming. I suppose everybody does that. I don't know, some people choose to say: "Oh no, she never screams this way. But I'm sure that they do." . . . You know how that is. It ain't that bad, so. . . . Definitely, we're confrontational. We don't keep anything down. If something is there you let it out. Get it out in the open. And then it'll be over with. You can be mad, but then that's not going to last that long. And then it'll be over with. And you start over again. Each day's a new day.

A 57-year-old African-American woman, Della, married thirty-seven years, described how it was and continues to be between her and Douglas:

> It was alright for him to have flaws, but me, I had to be perfect. Douglas somewhat felt that way when we first got married, that he was the man in the house. But I was the type of woman that would always say: "No, you're not. If I got to give in to things for you, you got to give in for me." And I stood on those grounds. You can't tell me what to do. If you don't want me to tell you what to do, then don't tell me; please, don't even waste your time. So that's why I say it's a lot of giving and a lot of taking in marriage. If you can dish it out, you got to be able to take it too. And today, I guess, I see a lot of women, they want things their own way. They don't want to do this, they don't want to do that . . . I always wanted to give a little and wanted to take some. But I didn't want that whole thing dumped on my shoulders where I have to be doing all the taking. He and I aren't people to give in or give up. We'll keep hammering at it. We always disagreed on that. Even 'til today, we do . . . . You just got to learn to say: "Hey, it just didn't work out," and not feel so hurt over it. Maybe I'm just one of those people like that. If it didn't work out, I can't convince him; I can't keep on banging my head up against the wall because you don't agree with things that I agree with.

Dynamic tension in confronting differences continued to characterize African-American marriages through the parenting years. In that respect, African-American couples were quite different from other couples. While the significant differences between African Americans and others disappeared during the post-parenting years, African Americans continued to report higher levels of confrontation in their relationships.

Protestants recalled more confrontation in their early relationships (65 percent) than either Catholics (42 percent) or Jews (30 percent) [X^2 (2, N = 120) = 9.19, p = .01]. Although several white Protestants reported confrontational relationships similar to those of African Americans, the African Americans contributed significantly to that finding since 82 percent of African Americans were Protestant. Perhaps, as we observed in Chapter 1, Protestants, whether white or black, entered marriage with less sense of who they were to be in their relationships. When behaviors were not ascribed as they were for Jewish and Mexican-American couples, negotiations were required to work out mutually acceptable roles. As couples struggled to clarify gender-related behaviors appropriate to their relationships, conflict was a result especially in relationships where expectations were ambiguous or incompatible. Conversely, internalized ascriptions of one's role which were syntonic with the expectations of the spouse may have neutralized conflict.

Modes of Avoidance

Although styles of confrontation varied somewhat, there was a generic quality to that mode of adaptation which was captured in the expression: "Let's talk!" Avoidance, on the other hand, was manifested in many forms: flight from face-to-face encounters, disarming the spouse, gunny sacking by reaching into the past to avoid current differences, alcoholism, and suppression.

Allison, a 56-year-old college-educated woman, recalled how her husband used flight to avoid having a fight with her:

> If ever I wanted to argue—this is in our beginning years—if I had something I was harping on and I wanted to argue, I mean he could see I was ready to pick a fight, he would go in his workshop in the basement. . . . If ever we wanted to argue, I'd just about say: "Don't run away; I want to finish this conversation." And he would be downstairs already, like forget it. Forget it!

The pattern of confrontative-avoidant complementarity in their marriage began to change after Allison threw a milk bottle at Arthur, the symbolic impact of which enabled him to recognize the problem.

A second mode of avoidance employed by some husbands was through commenting on a vulnerable spot within their wives' psyches. This had a disarming effect on the confrontational mode of the wife. In the following excerpt, Felicidad commented on the personal effect of her spouse's use of this defense:

> Sometimes my husband, if he really wants to shut me up and control me, he'll tell me that I'm starting to look and sound like my mother. That will shut me up for sure.

This is an interesting comment on how an unempathic confrontation, whether or not accurate, may have been used in the interest of avoidance. A similar remark framed by acceptance and empathy may have elicited a very different response from Felicidad. Such a remark, when motivated out of defensiveness and directed at a vulnerable spot in the spouse, had the effect of neutralizing face-to-face discussions of differences.

A closely related mechanism was that of gunny sacking in which an individual reached back to the past to avoid the present. When these memories were verbalized to the spouse, the effect was identical to the disarming defense. A 50-year-old woman, Evelyn, who had been married twenty-eight years, described the process of her spouse, Earl, reaching into his sack of memories and its effects on her:

> When he is in an argument, he likes to bring up the past. That I don't like. I feel the past is the past. I think it is unfair. Then you get off of the argument and try to defend the past. If I could change one thing about him, that would be it. When I say "the past," I mean some little thing I might have done or said. We all make mistakes, and you have to go on from that and live and grow from it. If it keeps being brought up, it is detrimental to growth. I wish he understood that about me.

Although we did not specifically ask about the use of alcohol or other substances as modes of avoidance, several individuals volunteered the information that alcohol had affected their lives and the quality of their marriages. One out of six marriages was affected adversely by alcohol abuse at some time, usually during the early years. Of the twelve respondents who reported drinking problems, ten were men. Since those reports were volunteered and not elicited, they may not be a reliable indicator of the use of alcohol as an avoidant defense. When it was mentioned, alcohol was depicted as a mode of avoidance. Eugene, 70 years of age and married twenty-two years, talked of his use of alcohol as an avoidant defense:

> I'm a person that . . . I take it and whitewash it. I apologize for it now but back then I felt like: "The hell with this mess, let me go get a drink."

One of the most common manifestations of avoidant behavior, especially among men, was suppression of thoughts and feelings. People talked of "keeping things in, of not expressing their feelings, of biting their tongues and of clamming up." To the spouse, suppression was not as offensive as other avoidant defenses. Suppression, an inner form of flight, was not tinged with overt anger toward the spouse as was disarming and gunny sacking. Kent, a 45-year-old college graduate, married for twenty years, described this mode of avoiding conflict which he contrasted with that of his spouse:

> I avoid conflict, but I won't allow silence, if you know what I mean . . . I avoid confrontation . . . She's more of an outgoing person; see, I hold in. I admit I hold in a lot, whereas she doesn't hold anything in. I mean, you can see the difference.

Change in Handling Conflict

As marriages evolved from their beginnings, through child-rearing, and into the post-parenting years, changes occurred in modes of handling differences. Although a slight shift was found in both spouses toward increased confrontation during the parenting years [$X2\,(1, N = 120) = 12.04$, $p = < .001$], a dramatic change was found as people lived out their lives together after rearing their children [$X^2\,(1, N = 120) = 10.28, p = .001$]. By the third phase of marriage, almost half of husbands and more than three fourths of wives utilized confrontation as their primary means of resolving differences. These figures represented a 15 percent increase in confrontational modes of handling differences for both spouses. For most couples, the process of change was toward mutuality of confronting differences during the empty-nest phase. The change created a new homeostasis within relationships. Cathy, married twenty-five years, described the change in her and Calvin:

> In the beginning, I could not express my feelings at all and there were a few times where I got very upset. Could not tell you what I was upset about. One time he sat with me for two hours just saying, "Just try and tell me what

is wrong." I could not get the words out. I think now that if he hadn't really spent a lot of time with me, what would have happened? But he helped me. Now it's sort of the opposite. I'm more expressive than he is sometimes, and sometimes he will clam up and he won't tell me and I know it's something that I did that he did not like and he thinks I should know what I did. Then you start playing a game. Sometimes I have to say, "Well, if I don't get it out of him, it won't be very pleasant." So I make the effort. I tended to think about things a little bit.... I'm not as quiet as he is now. I tend to be a little more fiery, but I hope that I have a bit of common sense to bring to the problem.

Although the findings suggest that predominant methods of handling interpersonal differences did not change for most husbands and wives as their marriages evolved, a significant minority of individuals changed toward mutually confrontational modes of resolving conflict and handling differences during the empty-nest years. The data also suggest that the changes were of a reciprocal nature. That is, both spouses needed to make shifts in their modes of handling differences if the changes were to be adaptive.

From the perspective of spouses observing the other spouses' behavior rather than their own behavior (on which the above discussion is based), we found a striking confluence in the data. Those observations were very similar to the observations of respondents about their own modes of handling differences. Thus, in the beginnings of these marriages, 75 percent of the husbands remembered their wives as confrontational and 77 percent of wives remembered their husbands as avoidant [X^2 (1, N = 120) = 32.04, p = < .001]. The comparable percentages reported earlier for self-observations were 62 percent for wives who recalled themselves as confrontational and 68 percent for husbands who recalled themselves as avoidant. The closeness in self and spousal observations continued through parenting and into the empty-nest years. In that phase, 83 percent of husbands reported their wives as confrontational; 58 percent of wives reported their husbands as avoidant [$X2$ (1, N = 120) = 22.22, p = .001]. Slight variations in these observations were attributable to men viewing themselves as more confrontational than their wives' perceptions of them, and women viewing themselves as less confrontational than their husbands' perceptions of them.

The conflicts of these couples were not substantially different from those of many couples whom we have treated in marital therapy for over thirty years. Unlike the latter, however, conflicts were contained at tolerable levels, and ways of handling conflict did not undermine or destroy marital alliances. Several factors may have been of critical importance in that process: each eventually defined and accepted the nature of conflicts in a similar way; at some level, they acknowledged asymmetrical modes of coping with or defending against these conflicts even though that rapprochement often did not occur until the post–child-rearing years; some had the capacity to observe their avoidant defenses and the motivation to modify their behavior. Most spouses also retained a strong commitment to their marriage and rarely considered divorce as an option for solving marital conflict. Commitment to the marriage, which was reinforced by internalized values of a cultural and religious nature, was critical, as was a hope that the relationship would improve. Finally, methods of handling differences, whether or not those changed, were part of a process that included several other dynamics which did change as these marriages matured. Some of these dynamics have been discussed already. They included a shift in husbands toward expressivity which enhanced communication between spouses. Relationship values such as trust, respect, understanding, and sensitivity were critical resources that appeared to ensure stability and enhance satisfaction. Finally, the sense of intimacy deepened as individuals grew older, a dynamic to be discussed in the next chapter.

The consequences of life crises cannot be underestimated in trying to understand these changes. Occasionally, a major medical problem precipitated the shift. For others, change was related to loss or impending loss of a career through retirement, especially since work was a powerful variable in defining identity among men. More frequently, change was part of a process that began during earlier phases. Sometimes, the youngest child growing to maturity or leaving the home became a catalyst for husband and wife to negotiate a transition to a new marital structure. The reciprocal nature of these changes was as important as the individual shifts themselves. That is, women may have been ready to enjoy a new level of relatedness. During the parenting years, investment in the marriage may have been compromised by the need to focus on children, especially during their adolescence which were stressful years for most couples. The data suggest that adolescence was as much a turning point for these marriages as it was for children who were negotiating the transition from childhood to adulthood. These family changes may have propelled couples to seek a new plateau of connectedness. Although that theme was found among these couples, it may lead to further estrangement in marriages not grounded on mutuality of commitment and of relationship values.

SUMMARY

Marital conflict is inevitable no matter how well prepared individuals are for marriage or how well they fit together as a couple. The conflicts of these couples did not appear to us to be more serious than those in most marriages and indeed did not result in major disruptions. Based on our evaluations of what individuals reported, major conflicts were found in 13 percent of marriages during the beginning phase. Most frequently, the focus of conflict involved difficulties in negotiating marital roles and responsibilities. Except for Jewish and Mexican-American couples where relative clarity and mutual acceptance of marital roles existed, negotiating roles and responsibilities was a focal conflict early in these marriages. Among Mexican-American, African-American, and blue-collar white couples, poverty and low wages were other sources of stress that contributed to conflict. When racism was reported as having an effect on marriage, it tended to bring spouses together rather than to produce conflict.

The most conflictual period in the life histories of these marriages was during the parenting years, especially the adolescence of children, when major conflict was reported by 30 percent of couples. Discipline of children was the principal source of conflict, along with a sense of disaffection from the spouse. That change in relatedness was reported more frequently by women than men but was unrelated to the educational level, ethnicity, or religious identification of respondents. After the children were grown and couples were alone again, conflict of a major nature was reported by 7 percent of couples. Conflict then reflected residuals of unresolved issues from earlier periods. Differences generated by conflict were not handled the same way by husbands and wives. Throughout marriage, men were more avoidant than women in dealing with conflicts. These gender-related modes of handling conflict persisted, although both husbands and wives changed considerably. By the empty-nest phase, almost half the men and over three-quarters of the women then resolved differences by face-to-face discussion.

REFERENCES

Demment, C. C. (1992). Marital satisfaction: A qualitative analysis. Unpublished doctoral dissertation, Boston College.

Hamel, C. (1993). Marital stability: A qualitative psychological study of African American couples. Unpublished doctoral dissertation, Boston College.

Hyde, J. S., & Phillis, D. E. (1979). Androgyny across the life span. *Developmental Psychology, 15*(3), 334–336.

Kanter, L. (1993). Marital stability: A qualitative psychological study of Jewish couples. Unpublished doctoral dissertation, Boston College.

Kayser, K. (1993). *When love dies: The process of marital dissatisfaction.* New York: Guilford Press.

Komarovsky, M. (1962). *Blue-Collar Marriage.* New York: Vintage Books.

Levinson, D. (1986). A concept of adult development. *American Psychologist, 41* (1), 3–13.

Lewis, J. M. (1988). The transition to parenthood: Stability and change in marital structure. *Family Process, 27,* 149–165.

McGee, J., & Wells, K. (1982). Gender typing and androgyny in later life. *Human Development, 25,* 116–139.

Mengden, S. (1994). Marital stability: A qualitative psychological study of Mexican American couples. Unpublished doctoral dissertation, Boston College.

Nadelson, C. C., Polonsky, D. C., & Matthews, M. A. (1984). Marriage as a developmental process. In C. C. Nadelson & D. C. Polonsky (Eds.), *Marriage and divorce: A contemporary perspective* (pp. 127–141). New York: Guilford Press.

O'Neil, J. M., Fishman, D. M., & Kinsella-Shaw, M. (1987). Dual-career couples' career transitions and normative dilemmas: A preliminary assessment model. *The Counseling Psychologist, 15* (1), 50–96.

Podbelski, J. J. (1993). Factors involved in marital stability. Unpublished doctoral dissertation, Boston College.

Rubin, L. B. (1976). *Worlds of pain.* New York: Basic Books.

Zube, M. (1982). Changing behavior and outlook of aging men and women: Implications for marriage in the middle and later years. *Family Relations, 31,* 147–156.

—4—

Intimacy

... I would be perfectly satisfied to sit in a room with her all day long
... I just like her to be next to me, near me ...

Erickson (1963) proposed that intimacy was one of the central developmental challenges of adulthood. With the consolidation of ego identity after adolescence, an individual was ready to lose the self again in adult relationships in which physical and psychological boundaries were relaxed. That concept of intimacy was based on the hypothesis that one had to possess a firm sense of self, which included stable ego boundaries, before one was ready to risk involvement in close adult relationships such as marriage.

Research supports a consensus about the importance of intimacy to the vitality of marital relationships, although there is no general agreement about its definition. Most frequently, intimacy has been used synonymously with personal disclosure (Jourard, 1971), which involves "putting aside the masks we wear in the rest of our lives" (Rubin, 1983, p. 168). To be intimate is to be open and honest about levels of the self that usually remain hidden in daily life. The extent of personal disclosure is proportionate to how vulnerable one allows the self to be with a spouse in revealing inner thoughts and feelings that usually are not apparent in social roles and behaviors of everyday life (Bowen, 1978; Masterson, 1985; Winnicott, 1965).

Intimacy also has been thought of as companionship (Lauer, Lauer, & Kerr, 1990; Sitton & Rippee,1986) and emotional bonding (Johnson & Greenberg, 1987). Others have defined intimacy as a process that changes as marriages mature (White et al., 1986). Schaefer and Olson (1981) considered intimacy to be a dynamic process that included emotional, intellectual, social, and cultural dimensions.

Our understanding of intimacy was based on explorations of several aspects of marital relationships which included variables discussed in previous chapters such as communication, relational values (trust, under-standing, respect, and sensitivity), modes of handling differences (avoid-ance to confrontation), and roles (expressive to instrumental). Intimacy consisted of a mutuality of understanding, acceptance, trust, and respect based on an openness and honesty of feelings between spouses manifested in physical, emotional, intellectual, and/or sociocultural dimensions of their lives together.

In this chapter, intimacy is explored from three perspectives: psychologi-cal intimacy, which includes emotional, intellectual, and social dimensions; sexual intimacy, which includes sexual intercourse as well as other behav-iors such as touching; and the interrelationship of psychological and sexual intimacies.

PSYCHOLOGICAL INTIMACY

Respondents talked of experiencing psychological intimacy when they were able to share their inner thoughts and feelings that were accepted, if not understood, by the spouse. Such experiences resulted in a sense of genuine connectedness and mutuality and might occur during sexual inter-course, as part of everyday interactions, or while participating together in a social or cultural event. A couple in their fifties reflected on what intimacy meant to them. She described her husband as

My best friend, best lover. The person I can come home to when something bad happens to me. Unfortunately, we have not had parents for many years. He is my parent as well as my friend. He is the person who most cares what is happening to me. The same as in the past. There is not a morning where he does not say, "Oh, you look nice today." He says it with such sincerity that I know he means it.

The meaning of intimacy to him was as follows:

I don't like to have my own space. You might as well be by yourself . . . the important thing is to like being with the other person. I would be perfectly satisfied to sit in a room with her all day long. I just like her to be next to me, near me. If you don't have that feeling, I think there is a piece that is missing. I think we are our own people, but we do it together. You just have to respect the other person . . . trust their decisions and beliefs and want to be with them.

In contrast to the frequency of sexual intercourse which declined as people grew older, the quality of psychological intimacy was enhanced during the empty-nest years. Individuals reported increasing satisfaction with the psychological dimensions of their relationships after children left home. One-half of all respondents, divided equally between men and women, recalled the early years of their marriages with a sense of psychological intimacy. The other half talked of memories which reflected little or mixed intimacy. There was a slight decline during the child-rearing years. However, during the empty-nest years, seven out of ten wives and a slightly higher number of husbands described their marriages in psychologically intimate terms.

The quality of intimacy changed as spouses grew older together. Sometimes, the change was difficult to capture with words. This 60–year-old skilled tradesman talked of the change in the quality of intimacy:

I don't believe that people who know us would say that we're anything but very close . . . we have a good relationship. We show it. It's not in a showy sort of a way but I think . . . just the way I treat her . . . I can't say we're closer; I think we're comfortable . . . not meaning that it's like an old pillow or something else like that. We can do things that we couldn't do before. I could call her up and say: "Do you want to go out and eat?" not worrying whether she's going to have to get dinner for the kids . . . it makes it a lot easier in the communication part . . . it's different. I can't say it's better because I've always enjoyed life, but maybe looser is a good word for it.

For others, the nature of intimacy in the empty-nest years was interrelated with the changes of growing older. Individuals needed each other in ways that were often different from earlier periods. An African-American woman, whose marriage of forty years was quite conflictual, talked of change in the quality of intimacy:

You got to really cleave to one another. . . . I need lots of tender, loving care now, more so than I did when I was younger. When I was younger, I didn't need so much. But I need a lot of understanding now, and a lot of TLC, and he does too. I notice that about him since he's gotten older. . . . Whereas years ago when our children were growing up and he was stronger, he didn't need all this love and all this TLC, but he does now. And he'll let you know it: "I need my time for you to just rub my bald head."

Several other themes emerged from the data which contribute to an understanding of how these people experienced psychological intimacy. First, the level of intimacy changed throughout each of the three phases of marriage. Often, crises or problems were turning points in the development of psychological intimacy. Changing circumstances, such as the children leaving home, also left room for a shift in the quality of relationships during the empty-nest years. Second, meanings associated with psychological intimacy varied only slightly by gender. In many marriages, wives took the lead role in nurturing the development of psychological intimacy. In that respect, women talked more about marital relationships in holistic terms which included behavioral as well as relational dynamics. Third, Mexican Americans compared to others reported higher levels of psychological intimacy throughout the three phases of marriage ($p = < .01$).

Intimacy as Process

A couple in their early seventies talked of the sense of psychological intimacy throughout their forty-five year marriage. Freeman expressed how he felt about the changes that occurred between him and his wife, Fannie:

As far as the two of us, I always felt very caring and very warm toward her and still do . . . I liked her so much that nothing she could have done could get in the way of things . . . I can't explain it really; I just liked the girl. We've been married for forty-five years now, and I feel closer to her than I've ever felt. I mean, mentally and physically and really, if ever two people have ever blended beautifully, she and I have blended, in my own mind anyway.

We've had our problems . . . we became closer when she had the miscarriages. I was more supportive of her and maybe she leaned on me more in those years. When things were bad in the store, I'd come home and cry on her shoulder a little bit; I don't mean cry, you know, discuss it with her, and she was very supportive of me in those years; maybe some of these different problems that we had over the years have brought us closer together and more dependent upon each other.

Freeman identified several components of psychological intimacy which, in one form or another, were evident in the responses of others.

Feelings of warmth and closeness were prominent themes, as was the sense of safety to be one's self within the relationship. Intimacy developed when each spouse could rely on the other for understanding and support. It was not unusual for respondents to comment on problems which included miscarriages, illnesses, and deaths of loved ones as turning points in developing interpersonal closeness and mutuality. Although there were many similarities in how Fannie thought of intimacy, she viewed some aspects differently from Freeman:

> We got along fine through the three different phases.... At first there was the love and the excitement, sex and love, and everything.... The best stage of our lives is right now. I'm really enjoying it being the two of us: he really is my very best friend.... During the time of the children, probably, was hard because I was a very nervous mother.... What was really good was that even at times when I was not talking, I always knew that Freeman was really there for me. Always. And sometimes I used to get angry with myself because I knew what I was doing and still couldn't seem to not do it. I think all the things we actually shared together and went through.... I had a couple of misses that were not easy ones.... brought us together even more.

Fannie implied that the transition into the post-parenting years had a positive effect on their relationship. Because parenting had been a stressful period for her, she, like several other respondents, reinvested in the marital relationship at a different level. No doubt, the continuity of mutual caring and support present in their relationship throughout the earlier years offered them a solid base on which to renegotiate their relationship.

For Ignacio and Isabel, a Mexican-American couple, themes of distance and separateness characterized the marriage. Ignacio's work took him away from the family, which served to neutralize marital conflict. He was constantly angry at Isabel for what both acknowledged was a difficulty on her part in expressing her love for him; he had a mistress. The death of one of their children was a turning point in the development of their relationship. Each spouse changed in small ways, which facilitated connectedness. As with most respondents, these modifications were in an adaptive direction. Isabel spoke to the above themes:

> I'm the kind of person who doesn't know how to show my love, and this is something that he and I would sometimes fight about because he'd say that I never tell him I love him and I'd say that he knows I do, but he wants me to tell him and he's always telling me and touching me and hugging me. I don't know what it is about me, but I tell him that's the way I am, and you're just

going to have to take it, that's the way I am. I know we've gotten closer. Like I say, we talk more than we did. At first, we didn't used to and he would say you should have told me this and that, but now. I think it's been good. I think losing my son brought us closer. I really do.

Ignacio reported:

The death of my kid changed our marriage. I don't know. It was rough. I guess it brought us closer together. I really do. There was a point before that happened ... where I didn't want to be with her. I was getting involved with someone else. I woke up when we lost the kid; we got closer, real close. She forgave me for doing what I was doing.

Tragedy and loss were themes in the marriages of these two couples. Prior to the miscarriages, Freeman and Fannie felt positively about their marriage. Their feelings for one another were resources in coping with those losses. Ignacio and Isabel had a more precarious relationship before the death of their son. Unlike Freeman and Fannie, they could not rely on a history of positive feelings to help them through the tragedy. Yet, both couples emerged from these experiences with feelings of mutual closeness. Turning points reinforced feelings of intimacy already present in marriages, as with Freeman and Fannie, or acted as a catalyst for couples to find a new level of intimacy, as with Ignacio and Isabel.

Growing older changed perspectives on love and relationships for several individuals. Frequently, respondents commented on changes in psychological intimacy during the empty-nest years compared to earlier times in their marriages. Individuals often used words such as "best friend" to describe what their spouses meant to them. These words and their synonyms may suggest that parts of the self, obscured by the pressures of earlier periods, emerged within the safety of loving relationships during the post-parenting years. The qualitative changes in intimacy need to be understood within the context of other changes that were occurring as marital relationships evolved. It is possible that the requirements of parenting and other work roles acting together with developmental forces compromised psychological intimacy during earlier periods of these marriages. In previous chapters, we discussed how modes of handling differences were modified as couples grew older when both husbands and wives became more confrontational in the post-parenting years. Handling differences through face-to-face discussion rather than through avoidance nurtured the development of psychological intimacy. Similarly, increased understanding and sensitivity were reported as marriages matured. These developments, together with constancy of trust and respect, also nurtured a sense of psychological intimacy.

Gender and Intimacy

Orientation to and behavior within relationships are different for men and women. Women may define themselves within relationships and experience security in continuity of attachments. For men, relatedness may be valued as a means to an end which may be realized through a relationship. Studies have found that wives were better at the empathic aspects of relationships than were husbands. Thus, it was reasonable to expect significant differences between husbands and wives in how each valued and perceived marital intimacy.

Although differences were apparent between husbands and wives as they talked about psychological intimacy, these differences were not as distinct as developmental research suggested. In part, the variations by gender may have reflected how individuals perceived and valued different components of psychological intimacy within themselves and in the spouse. The observations of a couple illustrated those differences. Joseph, a 57-year-old Jewish male married to Julia for thirty-two years, saw her as

> Very, very supportive of everything I did ... a big factor in my getting to where I am and, I think, that had a lot to do with our marriage being successful. She was very unselfish, and she would sacrifice so that I could go out and do my thing. One thing that Julia and I have always done, always, is talk constantly, to each other. I don't know what we talk about, and I don't know what we've had to talk about all these years, but we still communicate with each other ... for some reason, we can just communicate. We've had fights ... when she gets mad at me, I stop talking to her. And then she feels very bad, and this may last a day or two, and then it passes and everything is fine again.... She's more open than I am. I keep a lot inside. I appear to be very laid back and easy-going. I'm not. I keep a lot inside and I don't let it out, and that's probably not good. But that's the way I am. It's good now. Now is great.

Many men viewed observable qualities in their wives, such as support, as important in developing a sense of psychological intimacy in their marriages. Women, on the other hand, often commented on the observable and then went on to identify their understanding of the underlying dynamics that shaped behavior. More than men, women talked about the interplay of relational dynamics. For example, Julia reported that

I filled certain needs in him, and I know he filled certain needs in me. He needed some direction, which I think he looked to me for ... he didn't have very high self-esteem. I may have boosted his confidence a lot ... He tells me I go ballistic over, you know, stupid things, and he outwardly is very calming, but if you asked who was more nervous, I would have to say he is. It just doesn't show ... we're very good friends. I don't always agree with him, and he does not always agree with me, and we'll take two very different approaches sometimes on an issue, but we are good friends and I know he's there for me, and I know I'm there for him. And that's the way it's really always been.... We're good friends. I get ticked sometimes and so does he at things. But we're good friends through it all, and I think that if you have a good friend, you should be able to disagree, or agree, or get angry or be happy or any number of emotions, if that's your friend, that's your friend.... You know, the bad things seem awful, but there are a lot more good times. Through it all, I don't even know how to describe it, you just have that closeness ... there has to be enough there so that when all these little outside things are finally gone, it's not: "Who are you? I don't know you, and we don't have anything." You have to really work at keeping that level of a relationship active. There has to be enough of a spark there, not just a physical spark, but just the whole picture.

Themes of connectedness and separateness were important dynamics in understanding how intimacy developed in various marriages. For some respondents, connectedness was highly valued and central to their sense of marital intimacy. For others, being connected along with a need to be separate was important. As spouses grew older, they talked in similar terms about psychological intimacy, with themes of connection being dominant over separation.

Ethnicity and Intimacy

Of the four independent variables in this study (gender, education, religion, and ethnicity), only ethnicity was related significantly to psychological intimacy throughout the three phases of marriage. Eighty-three percent of Mexican Americans, 46 percent of whites, and 39 percent of African Americans spoke of their early relationships as intimate [X^2 (4, N = 120) = 12.97, p =.01]. After a slight decrease during the parenting years, reports of marital relationships as psychologically intimate rose dramatically in the empty-nest years. During that phase, all Mexican Americans compared to seven out of ten other respondents described their marriages in psychologically intimate terms [X^2 (4, N = 120) = 12.74, p = < .01]. Although these findings may have resulted, in part, because of the connotations of words such as intimacy to Mexican Americans and others, they were more likely related to real differences between the groups. Nonetheless, Mexican Americans talked in less ambivalent terms about the intimate aspects of their current relationships than did whites or African Americans.

As Falicov (1982) has noted, one needs to distinguish between observable characteristics that are attributed to the social behavior of a group and individual characteristics that may apply within a family. A 56-year-old Mexican-American woman commented on such an observation as it applied to the public and private aspects of her husband's behavior:

> I can tell you that Mexican men are not affectionate outside the house. They're cold and they're the macho men. They're very affectionate inside the house. They're very affectionate, and yet you see them out in public and they're not.... I'll give you a handle on that. We've been married thirty-five years ... even when we were dating, he has never forgotten a birthday, Christmas, Valentine's, any anniversary or holiday.... The card may look like the dickens, but there's a card. See, that's how sensitive they are. And you see them and you would never dream they were that type, never! They are cold and crude and, but they're not. Especially with the children, and the babies, they just melt and they take care of them.... To see him, you'd never detect that in him. He looks so cold and crude.... We've always saved one evening for us. . . . We had to do this; otherwise, we never had time for ourselves.... We've always made time for us ... I think you get closer. The biggest burden he worries about is financial security ... instead of a strain, I think we got closer because I would try to make things more comfortable, try to soften that blow of financial strain.

In the context of family and church, Mexican-American couples felt supported in developing and maintaining intimacy. Similar resources may have been important to other couples, but Mexican Americans talked explicitly about church and family. Armando described the role of the church in helping with problems that undermined intimacy:

> We talk together now, but before we didn't ... if we had this preparation for marriage like we have now, Alicia and I would have known ourselves better than what we did ... when I went the wrong way, we couldn't talk like we do now ... It's important when things start to go, that you talk to someone about it ... to sponsors or someone in the church like me and my wife are now, someone that's experienced. Someone that has more years.

Alicia commented on the significance of family to their sense of intimacy:

We have a large group, a lot of people all the time. I think it's made us grow closer because Armando and I just go into our room and close the door and find time for ourselves . . . I think it's helped us. It's helped the kids bond together ... they help each other. We have a close-knit family, sometimes too close.

Closeness that was often inseparable from family cohesiveness was a prominent theme among Mexican-American couples. Although marital intimacy was important, it was also a means of nurturing the bond among family members. Religion and the church were important resources for couples in developing and maintaining marital and familial cohesiveness.

SEXUAL INTIMACY

Although respondents attached less importance to sexual intercourse and found it less satisfying as they grew older, sexual relations remained important and satisfying from the beginning through the post-parenting years. Those trends were accompanied by a decrease in the frequency of sexual intercourse especially during the empty-nest years. In the child-rearing phase, sex became less satisfying for wives who also thought of sex as less important once they had children; twice as many women as men said that sexual intercourse was not important during the parenting years. Although sex became less satisfying as people aged, it remained an important part of a majority of marriages. During the empty-nest years, sexual relations were less than satisfying for 45 percent of the respondents, a trend that was accompanied by a decline in the frequency of sexual intercourse. The physical demonstration of affection, especially touching, was constant for about half of the couples throughout the three phases of marriage. The physical expression of affection was most characteristic of Mexican Americans, a difference that became more pronounced as couples grew older ($p = < .01$).

Seventy-five percent of the respondents felt positively about their sexual relationships in the beginning years of marriage. This theme was reflected in the observations of a 54-year-old white male, married for twenty-nine years:

This has been excellent from the very beginning. . . . Very satisfactory sex life ... we are just fortunate that it worked out that way. It won't work out unless you work at it and have consideration.

His 52-year-old wife agreed with him:

It has been wonderful, gets better every year.

Their observations were typical of those respondents whose sexual relationships started and remained on a highly satisfying level. Other investigators (Lauer, Lauer, and Kerr, 1990) have found that satisfied spouses generally agree about the quality of their sexual relationships which was found among satisfied couples in this study. Most respondents who had a consistently satisfying sexual relationship felt that "good sex" was essential to a successful marriage, as articulated by Karen, a 51-year-old working woman with four children:

I think you need to have good sex to have a good marriage. No doubt about it. I think that when you've had a crummy, "stinken" day, that if you can have good sex, or even not sex, but to be able to snuggle up in bed, I think it is important. I can't imagine a couple that could have a marriage without good sex.

For those respondents, who experienced sexual difficulties in the early years of their marriages, openness to discussion and willingness to learn about one's self and spouse led to improved sexual relations and satisfaction. This was reflected in what Douglas, a 63-year-old African-American male, had to say about sexual relations:

When I was younger it was just bang, bang and that was the end of it. Now, we enjoy sex ... it goes along with marriage, and it helps a marriage. And the things we did, we talk about it many times and that really helped me a lot. It helped her too ... I really think it helped our sex life.

His wife, Della, of thirty-seven years agreed with him:

I'd say that our sex life improved, probably better now since we're older.

One out of four spouses expressed less than positive memories about their sexual relations during the early years of marriage. Debra, a 62-year-old homemaker with three children married for forty years, recalled:

Sex was never one of the strong points of our marriage. I don't know whose fault that was. He was always satisfied. I also felt, which wasn't his fault, I guess it was mine, that I was the wife and he was the husband, and if he wanted to have sex, then I should cooperate. So I went through the motions.

Couples whose unsatisfying sexual relations persisted accommodated to one another in several ways. Unlike spouses who were able to work at mutually agreeable solutions, these spouses continued to experience sex as unsatisfying. Not infrequently, the matter remained a "secret" between spouses as in the above relationship. That is, discussion about the lack of sexual satisfaction and about differences in sexual needs was avoided. Among some couples, avoidance was symptomatic of how they dealt with interpersonal conflicts. Lack of sexual relations was a manifestation of negative feelings about unmet emotional needs in the marriage. The observations of Ivan, a 48-year-old man, illustrated how spouses acted out interpersonal conflicts by withholding sex:

> There were times when we certainly punished each other by withholding sex. I mean if you're not talking, you're certainly not going to fool around. There were times when we just did not have sex, not for protracted periods of time, but certainly long enough that it was obvious that something was wrong. And, again, that's been cyclical.

Thirty-five percent of the respondents reported diminishing frequency and satisfaction with sex during the child-rearing years. During that phase, twice as many women as men remembered a lack of sexual satisfaction. Doreen, a 63-year-old woman with five children, recalled:

> Part of the problem was physical energy. I needed a lot of sleep ... as I was busy with the kids, made me tired, want to go to sleep. He could not understand that, and we basically drifted apart on any sexual relations. In the beginning, it was a very passionate relationship. Then, it became a question of energy.

A 67-year-old African-American woman, Beth, married for fifty years with four children, summed up the feelings of women who had to contend with the demands of children and their spouses:

> There are children and you got to choose. It's not that you love your husband less and that the husband loves the wife less.... He loves the wife more, but he doesn't seem to be getting all that he wants of the wife because the attention has gone to the child. Because you got to take care of that kid if you're going to be any kind of a mother. So there's got to be time sharing, and that can be hard for the man.

Our findings are similar to those of others who have studied sexuality between spouses during the child-rearing years. To the role of wife was added that of mother. Women discussed the physical and emotional demands and the major responsibilities they carried as mothers of growing children. Their transitions to parenthood were different from those of men (Feldman & Nash, 1984). There was an increase in marital stress for mothers compared with fathers (Miller & Sollie, 1980). Many wives felt emotionally drained and often overburdened (Bernard, 1974).

Sexual relations and satisfaction did not change for 65 percent of the respondents during the child-rearing years. A theme of working at ways of maintaining sexual satisfaction was evident as respondents talked of that period in their marriages. For example, Evelyn, a 50-year-old working mother of two children, recalled:

When the children were small, we set aside a time for ourselves. Usually on a Sunday night we would put the kids to bed early, then we would have a nice candlelight dinner and some wine. We really worked at getting together like that. We tried to go away once a year for an overnight.

Although the child-rearing years were often stressful and had the potential to undermine sexual relations as other researchers have found (Belsky, Spanier, & Rovine, 1983; Lewis, 1988), the majority of couples in this study remained sexually satisfied.

The Empty-Nest Years

During the empty-nest years, 55 percent of the respondents remained sexually active and satisfied. Although the frequency of sexual intercourse declined, individuals talked about a maturity in their sexual relationships. There were frequent references to an increase in feelings of caring and affection. The change in the frequency of sexual relations was portrayed by Emily, a 75-year-old woman married for fifty years:

Things are a lot different when you get older. It doesn't preclude that everything is gone. It's just that it's not as frequent . . . you taper off when you're older. It becomes different, but the affection is still there.

Men expressed similar observations to those of women. Greg, a 69-year-old husband of forty-seven years, commented on the change:

The frequency is slightly different, but it has been very good as far as I'm concerned . . . I think it's actually better than it was in the beginning. I'd say there is deeper affection in the past twenty years than there was in the first.

There's always been caring but even more so in the last half of our married life.

For several respondents, growing older represented a rebirth in sexual vitality. Without the children in the home there were more opportunities for spontaneity and discussion, which led to an increase in feelings of sexual satisfaction as well as emotional closeness. A 68-year-old woman, Fannie, with two children, addressed that theme:

I'll tell you, this old age is comfortable. There was a period when the kids were small, and I wasn't terribly interested in sex. But it came back, and it's fine.

Among 45 percent of respondents, there was a decline in the frequency of sexual relations and satisfaction. For several of those respondents, physical ailments associated with the aging process impaired sexual functioning. Some of the reported physical problems included diabetes, hysterectomies, heart attacks, arthritis, and surgical procedures which led to a general loss of sexual desire in women and impotence in men.

Several women described how hysterectomies affected their sexuality. A loss of sexual desire was recounted by Judy, a 56-year-old mother of six children:

When I was young, I thought I was really sexy. . . . But after I had my hysterectomy, I don't find myself as sexy. I know you're not supposed to say that, and I know that's not supposed to be true, but it's true . . . I don't have estrogen in my body and I can't take it because I have hypertension. I think it does change you. I think I'm less interested in sex than I was. So I just pretend I'm the same person. But it's not quite the same.

Heart disease affected the sexual functioning of several men. In discussing his reactions to a heart attack and his later impotency, Esteban, a 53-year-old Mexican American, observed:

As we get older, you just don't do that as much. Yes, you do hug her, but you don't kiss her like you did when you were younger . . . it has changed a lot.

Esperanza, his wife of thirty-one years, talked of the situation and how they coped:

Since he got sick we slowed down. I got used to living where we hardly have any sex . . . when we're talking about stuff like that, I kind of like to make a joke about how we live like brother and sister. And we don't mind now.

In discussing the infirmities of old age and its influence on sexual satisfaction, partners talked of sex as one part of their relationships, and not as more important than other elements. This theme was summarized by a 50-year-old woman, married for thirty-one years:

All the intimacy of a marriage is not necessarily intercourse. I think we base it on our intimacy in other ways. Right now there is no sexual contact. Just being able to hold each other is an important part of the relationship. Going to bed and cuddling, that is important. Holding each other also. They are all important parts of the relationship.

A common thread in many marriages was the substitution of other satisfying ways of expressing intimacy. A 48-year-old woman, married for twenty-six years, spoke of how physical affection compensated for a decline in sexual intercourse:

The only thing that I think is different is that I wish we were more sexually involved. I kind of miss that . . . but that is the only thing that I would say that I wish would be different, but if not, it's fine. I love him in sickness and in health, for richer or poorer. So it's fine. It has not affected our relationship with each other. We cuddle. We hug and kiss.

As their relationships matured, couples reported a change in sexuality which has also been found in other studies (Roberts, 1979). Physical touching replaced intercourse, and couples reported feeling an emotional connectedness to each other. There was a mutuality in the observations of both husbands and wives which was different from their observations about sex earlier in the marriages. That is, there were more similarities than differences in viewing the decline in sexual relations and the increase in psychological intimacy.

The Importance of Sexual Intimacy

The earlier discussion focused on how satisfied respondents felt about sexual relations. As noted, satisfaction and frequency of sexual intercourse were correlated, especially during the early years of marriage prior to children. Frequency of sex lessened during the parenting years and declined considerably in the post-parenting phase. As frequency dropped so did satisfaction. The importance of sexual relations followed a similar pattern. However, sex was still regarded as important among those respondents who did not consider it satisfying in the empty-nest years. Even when one could not function sexually as one had been able to previously, sex as a part of marriage was still important. The decline in sexual functioning was balanced by two other aspects of sexuality as spouses grew old together: psychological intimacy and physical expressions of affection (e.g., hugging and touching).

Before the arrival of children, 91 percent of the respondents talked of sex as being important in their relationships, a finding that did not vary significantly by gender, religion, ethnicity, or education. In other words, nearly everybody considered sex important in the early years of marriage. For the following couple, sex was important not only in the beginning of their marriage but also throughout the years. For this 63-year-old man, sex was

> Very important . . . you could say delightful! It's a fulfilling feeling. It certainly feeds your ego to know that you can turn somebody on, that they desire you . . . it strokes you. It's fun. It's recreational. . . . It beats bowling.

Though important for his wife, sex began to take on a different significance as they grew older. While she attached as much importance to sexual relations as he did in the early years, she commented:

> His sexual appetite goes on and on. I thought by the time he was 50, 55 I thought, Oh, it'll be all over. Oh my God! Oh brother!

Ian, a 64-year-old man, married for forty-one years with five children, used the following metaphor to convey what sex had meant to him throughout marriage:

> If all else fails, sex holds it together. It's the mortar that holds the brick.

The theme of sex not being so important was expressed by 9 percent of respondents and was illustrated by Kent, married for twenty-three years:

> It's strange, because I never considered that to be an important part of a marriage. I have said that before, and I say that to everyone. To me, that is not what makes or breaks a marriage. Again, that is probably old fashioned. To me, there is more to it, and to be a companion and to get along and take

care of raising a family and succeed in raising that family; that's what is important.

During the child-rearing years, twice as many women as men viewed sex as not being important. Several respondents described how their sexual relations changed while they were rearing their children. A 63-year-old woman recalled:

We basically drifted apart on any sexual relations. I had enough to do, and he accepted that, and it did not bother me.

A 69-year-old man remembered:

Children demand a lot of time, so you don't have a lot of time for yourself nor can you be as spontaneous. So, sex isn't as important.

As the frequency of sexual relations was compromised in the interest of caring for children, the importance of sex to many couples took on a meaning quite different from what it had had in the beginning of their relationships. For those couples, one way of adapting to that change was to regard sexual relations with less importance than in earlier years. For several, the change resulted in a lowering of satisfaction not only with sex but also with the marriage in general. For others, the child-rearing years did not compromise the frequency of and satisfaction with sex; they regarded sex as important, if not central, to a satisfying marital relationship.

By the third phase, the trend toward thinking of sex as less important continued. Seventy-three percent of wives and 82 percent of husbands then regarded sex as important, although 45 percent of both men and women did not find sex satisfying. Those who felt sex was important to their marriage reported having satisfying sexual relations. A common theme about the importance of sex for the majority of respondents was expressed by Earl, a 53-year-old male, married for twenty-eight years:

Sex is the nice stuff. I don't think we ever had problems sexually. Intimacy has always been open. We are able to talk about our feelings and needs.

A different theme became evident as individuals talked of sex in the third phase of marriage. Both males and females identified the strengthening of psychological intimacy which served as a balance to losses in sexual functioning. A 66-year-old woman, married for forty-three years, talked of love as a balance to a decline in sexual functioning:

We've always been in love. We're more in love now, and it just gets better and better.

Physical impairments, as noted earlier in this chapter, were commonly identified as reasons for change in sexual relations and satisfaction. Fred, 61years old and married thirty-seven years, had several heart attacks and discussed how he and his wife struggled with impotency:

Mentally the feelings were there, but sometimes physically I was just not able. She has been very understanding ... after you live with someone for such a long time, you can sense when somebody wants some affection of some kind ... I try the embracing and that type of thing, but as far as the actual act, forget it. It can't be consummated ... and she's very understanding about that. She has never brought it up to me that I can't deliver.

His 61-year-old wife, Fran, expressed her empathy for him and how her love enabled her to accept the change in their relationship:

We have been very compatible, and I feel badly for him ... I never disliked being with him ... and when you love somebody very much you adjust; that's what it's all about.

Those respondents who struggled with infirmities looked at their sexual relationships through different lenses. Sometimes, a theme of resignation was evident in their responses along with an acceptance of what they could not change. A 72-year-old woman offered the following reflection on the current state of her fifty-year marriage:

We don't have the kind of relationship the way I would like it to be, but it's not making me unhappy. I don't know how to explain it. I am accepting what I have. And I am saying to myself: Well, what am I going to try to change him for. He's been like this all the time. Why now? You've put up with this all these years, so you make the most with what you have now. You work for what you have now. So that's what I'm going to do.

In attaching a positive interpretation to a potentially negative situation, this woman used a strategy commonly helpful to respondents in similar circumstances. A theme of resignation and acceptance was evident in their responses. Others who struggled with a decline in sexual relations tried to find new meaning in their marital relationships. What emerged quite often for them was a sense of closeness that may have been dormant for several years.

Physical Affection

Compared to the frequency of sexual relations, physical intimacy without sexual intercourse remained more or less constant throughout the three phases of marriage; a slight decline was reported in the parenting phase. Fifty percent of respondents saw themselves as demonstrative with their spouses, a figure slightly higher for wives than husbands. Physically demonstrating affection was more characteristic of Mexican Americans than of others, a difference that became pronounced as couples grew older [X^2 (2, $N = 120$) = 13.25, $p = .001$]. Other studies have found that physical affection is valued highly in Mexican-American culture (Falicov, 1982; Vega, 1990; Williams, 1990).

The theme of physically demonstrating affection between Mexican-American spouses was expressed by Dora who had been married for twenty-six years:

> We're not ashamed of our love. Public displays of affection, we're not afraid to touch each other. We're always touching: at the movies, church, when we're laying down in bed, we're always touching each other. We hold hands when we walk together. A lot of people can't believe we've been married so long.

Those respondents, roughly half of the sample, who did not report as much demonstration of physical affection as this woman often referred to individual temperaments which may have been different from their spouses. The subject was typically discussed in terms of an individual's style or tendency not to be affectionate. For example, a 50-year-old woman, married for twenty-eight years, commented on the issue of touching in her marriage:

> I'm not a mushy-mushy, huggy-huggy person. I've never been mushy. I don't mind being hugged, but ... I like to be treated nice and with a lot of respect. I don't mind being hugged once in a while, but not all the time. That's just me.

A 56-year-old husband, married for twenty-nine years, commented on the theme:

> I'm not that way with holding hands or touching, or putting my arms around her. She always has been warmer. And at times, she voiced complaints about it. She has always been much more outwardly expressive.

Some couples identified their cultural backgrounds as influential in shaping how they were inhibited from expressing affection in a physical way. A 48-year-old Irish Catholic shared his struggles with touching:

> I had to learn to touch. We particularly did not touch in public. I mean ... it's that Irish Catholic upbringing that if you were out you certainly did not display any emotional affection. It wasn't acceptable.

As with other factors that contributed to or detracted from marital happiness, spouses learned to accept differences and to live with limitations in how affection was demonstrated, not blissful but good enough. That adaptation was expressed by Kim who had been married for twenty-three years:

> There was never a problem. We were not demonstrative. There were no public displays of affection and touching. He was never Mr. Affectionate ... it was adequate.

Spouses adapted to the absence of physical touching in their relationships in a number of ways. Commitment to, acceptance of, and sometimes resignation to differences in which positive factors compensated for lack of physical affection were important components of intimacy. Other aspects in relationships, such as a sense of respect from the spouse, balanced deficits in expressing affection in a physical manner.

Gender and Sexuality

Gender differences are clearly a factor in understanding sexuality in marital relationships (O'Neil, Fishman, and Kinsella-Shaw, 1987; Zube, 1982). At least in part, differences result from socialization to gender roles. Men are socialized to value autonomy and achievement through relationships, and women are socialized to develop mutually enhancing relationships (Gilligan, 1982; Miller, 1986; Surrey, 1984). We wondered whether these differences would be manifested in the ways in which husbands and wives talked about the meaning of sexual relations.

Compared to wives, husbands were more inclined to use sexual relations as a barometer of the health of marital relationships. A 45-year-old woman, Irene, married for twenty-six years, observed:

> Sex played a role in confirming our closeness and emotional bond. I think that he is very dependent on those feelings. Probably more so than it should

be ... I feel that men depend on the sexual relationships to say:... "Everything must be OK because our sexual life is good, so everything is ... OK." I think they allow that to be their yardstick whether things are good, bad, or indifferent.

Another woman commented on her perception of differences between the sexes. Her 64-year-old husband had described long-standing difficulties in their sexual relations, which he attributed to tensions caused by temperamental differences; they did not talk about these difficulties. His wife, Jill, observed:

Sex has been difficult ... men are much more fragile when it comes to sex than women. We never communicated, but who knew anything? So it took years of adjustment, but that, too, has gotten better ... if a woman doesn't have an orgasm, well, she doesn't have an orgasm. But if men can't get an erection they figure that it is the end; it was never going to happen again.... If women refuse, they take it personally. Their makeup is very different. I just think when it comes to sex, they are way more fragile.

Selective understanding was a strategy that individual spouses used to cope with conflict, not only about sex but also about other issues in these marriages. The effectiveness of this strategy was not necessarily grounded on accuracy or on consensual validation of the spouse. Rather, selective understanding was a mode of adaptation through which spouses accepted and explained the behaviors of their partners in terms of family histories, gender differences, and societal norms that made sense for them. As in these two marriages, individuals used this strategy to adapt to persistent differences with their spouses. Being able to attach meaning to such difficulties enabled people to contain marital conflict at a level that was tolerable. In several marriages, the use of selective understandings led to positive changes not only in sexual relations but also in other dimensions of relationships. In those situations, adaptation was more a matter of selective shifts in relationships than in sweeping changes. Usually, these shifts were gradual rather than dramatic.

Attitudes and values about sexuality were substantially influenced by early socialization, which included religious training. Gender differences were evident in what several respondents said about the relationships between sex in marriage and their backgrounds. Again, selective understanding was a valuable tool in adapting to potentially serious conflict. A 59-year-old male, George, married with four children, commented:

We had to work out some problems. She had some long-standing traditional thoughts about sex, and she still harbors a lot of those. You go with what you get, you can't be demanding. You got to think of the other person ...she was initially changing in the dark, in the corner, and that kind of stuff. That's the way she was brought up, and that's okay. You don't spend a lifetime in bed anyway ... she was quite afraid you know, very traditional, too much so.

His 55-year-old wife, Grace, said:

He is much more sexual than I am. I am more affectionate and need hugs and kisses and some nice things, and then you get me in the mood to be sexual. You can't just boom, boom, bang. It's just the difference between two people. He always said from the time we were first married that sex was a very small part of marriage and don't worry about it, boom, boom, boom. It should be more than that. Growing up I went to Catholic school and the nuns. I really loved the nuns, and they really did a good job on me. When I got married I was still a virgin ... I had different needs in terms of the sexual relationship.

More often than not, spouses talked of sex and psychological intimacy as separate yet interrelated dimensions of their relationships. Wives were more likely than husbands to talk of the inseparability of sexual and psychological intimacies, a difference evident in the preceding vignette. In expressing their thoughts about intimacy, respondents made a conceptual distinction between the two dimensions while acknowledging that the quality of sex was contingent on feelings of psychological closeness toward the spouse. That theme was apparent in the observations of the following couple. The wife observed:

I guess the aspect of our sexual relationship that I have the hardest time with is that I often feel ... why do I want to go to bed with somebody that I don't talk with much other than to go to bed with. You know, there were times in our life when we weren't doing much together. And I still feel that plays a big role in maybe my dissatisfaction with our sexual life ... the biggest problem or disappointment is that it's not a fuller relationship. When it's good, it's good. When I feel strained, I feel myself not wanting to be involved sexually. It's like, I don't want to be here, ya know? If you don't talk to me in the kitchen, don't talk to me in the bedroom ... it's had its ebbs and tides over the years.

Her husband commented on the interplay between the psychological and sexual dimensions in their relationship:

It was better to ... take the risk and talk about it than it was to sit and brood about it. We had the ability to get inside each other's head and screw each other around and ... have done it at different stages in our marriage. Probably a typical relationship. You have the ability to punish and hurt depending on how you feel at a given moment; we've certainly done our share of that. When she was less than happy with me, naturally you're less inclined to engage in sex. At that time, it becomes perfunctory ... it is, for me, as much a head trip as it is a physical trip. I think sex is psychological as much as it is physical ... at those times you do it, but you don't have the good feeling.

When it came to valuing the interdependence of the sexual and psychological dimensions of relationships, the differences between husbands and wives were a matter of degree. Women compared to men were more inclined to speak of the inseparability of the two dimensions throughout marriage. As these two vignettes illustrate, however, most spouses viewed sex within the context of relationships as a whole. As with several couples who had experienced sexual tensions and conflicts throughout their marriages, gender differences became less apparent during the empty-nest years.

SUMMARY

Intimacy has been discussed as the experience of being connected to one's spouse psychologically and physically. While the two dimensions of being intimate were differentiated conceptually, most respondents talked of them as interrelated parts of feeling as one, yet separate from the spouse. Seventy-five percent of respondents recalled active and satisfying sexual relations early in marriage. Frequency of sex declined slightly during the child-rearing years; among women satisfaction with sex also declined during that phase. By the empty-nest years, psychological intimacy increased between spouses as the frequency of and satisfaction with sexual relations decreased. Even though frequency of intercourse declined, 55 percent of husbands and wives reported satisfying sexual relations. Physically expressing one's affection to the spouse through hugging and touching remained constant compared to an increase in psychological intimacy and a decrease in sexual relations. In understanding sexuality, it was important to view it in the context of relationships as a whole. Many couples felt closer to each other while continuing to have an active sexual relationship as they grew old together. Others felt closer even when illness and bodily impairments eliminated or reduced sexual relations. For them, physical touching was a means of reinforcing emotional connectedness.

REFERENCES

Belsky, J., Spanier, G. B., & Rovine, M. (1983). Stability and change in marriage across the transition to parenthood. *Journal of Marriage and the Family, 45,* 567–577.

Bernard, J. (1974). *The future of marriage.* New York: World.

Bowen, M. (1978). *Family therapy in clinical practice.* New York: Jason Aronson.

Erikson, E. (1950). *Childhood and society.* New York: W. W. Norton.

Falicov, C. J. (1982). Mexican families. In M. McGoldrick, J. K. Pearce, & J. Giordant (Eds.), *Ethnicity and family therapy.* New York: Guilford Press.

Feldman, S. S., & Nash, S. C. (1984). The transition from expectancy to parenthood: Impact of the firstborn child on men and women. *Sex Roles, 11,* 61–78.

Gilligan, C. (1982). *In a different voice: Psychological theory and women's development.* Cambridge, MA: Harvard University Press.

Johnson, S., & Greenberg, L. (1987). Emotionally focused marital therapy: An overview. *Psychotherapy, 24* (38), 552–660.

Jourard, S. M. (1971). *Self-disclosure: An experimental analysis of the transparent self.* New York: Wiley-Interscience.

Kayser, K., & Himle, D. (1991). *Marital intimacy: A model for clinical assessment and intervention.* New York: The Haworth Press.

Lauer, R. H., Lauer, J. C., & Kerr, S. T. (1990). The long-term marriage: Perceptions of stability and satisfaction. *International Journal of Aging and Human Development, 31,* 189–195.

Leuers, J. (1988). The transition to parenthood II: Stability and change in marital structure. *Family Process, 27,* 273–283.

Masterson, J. (1985). *The real self: A developmental self and objects relations approach.* New York: Brunner/Mazel.

Miller, B. C., & Sollie, D. L. (1980). Normal stresses during the transition to parenthood. *Family Relations, 29,* 459–465.

Miller, J. B. (1986). *Toward a new psychology of women.* Boston: Beacon Press.

O'Neil, J. M., Fishman, D. M., & Kinsella-Shaw, M. (1987). Dual-career couples' career transitions and normative dilemmas: A preliminary assessment model. *The Counseling Psychologist, 15* (1), 50–96.

Roberts, W. L. (1979). Significant elements in the relationship of long-married couples. *International Journal of Aging and Human Development, 10*(3), 265–272.

Rubin, L. B. (1983). *Intimate strangers.* New York: Harper & Row.

Schaefer, M., & Olson, D. (1981). Assessing intimacy: The PAIR Inventory. *Journal of Marital and Family Therapy,* 47–59.

Sitton, S., & Rippee, E. (1986). Women still want marriage: Sex differences in lonely hearts advertisements. *Psychological Reports, 58* (1), 257–258.

Surrey, J. (1984). The "self-in-relation": A theory of women's development. *Work in Progress #13.* Wellesley, MA: Stone Center Working Papers Series.

Vega, W. A. (1990). Hispanic families in the 1980's: A decade of research. *Journal of Marriage and the Family, 52,* 1015–1024.

White, K., Speisman, J., Jackson, D., Bartis, S., & Costos, D. (1986). Intimacy, maturity and its correlation in young married couples. *Journal of Personality and Social Psychology, 50,* 152–162.

Williams, N. (1990). *The Mexican American family: Tradition and change.* Dix Hills, NY: General Hall, Inc.

Winnicott, D. W. (1965). *The maturational process and the facilitating environment.* New York: International Universities Press.

Zube, M. (1982). Changing behavior and outlook of aging men and women: Implications of marriage in the middle and later years. *Family Relations, 31,* 147–156.

—5—

Decision Making

. . . you talk about it and sometimes your idea wins out and sometimes his idea wins out. It all depends . . .

The post–World War II decades witnessed dramatic shifts in male and female relationships, both at work and at home. Career patterns that were altered permanently during the war, opportunities for higher education regardless of gender, the civil rights movement which heightened awareness of inequalities for many groups, and the women's movement affected the relationships of males and females. Those social changes had an impact on American marriages, especially on the decision-making behaviors of husbands and wives (Bjorksten & Stewart, 1984; Prochaska & Prochaska, 1978; Reibstein, 1988; White, 1990).

Research focused on decision making in marriage has been built on Blood's pioneering work in the 1950s and 1960s (Blood, 1969). He developed a typology of marriages based on the power structure of relationships. Power was defined as the perception of who has the most influence in making decisions that affect a couple. Based on measurements of dominance and submission between spouses as they made decisions about a wide range of topics, three types of marital relationships were hypothesized: wife dominant/husband submissive, husband dominant/wife submissive, and the egalitarian relationship in which decision making was negotiated democratically between spouses. Based on that framework, findings on marital power were relatively consistent through the 1970s and 1980s: wife dominant/husband submissive couples were most likely to be unhappy; egalitarian couples reported the highest levels of marital satisfaction; and husband dominant/wife submissive couples fell in between these two categories (Bean, Curtis, & Marcum, 1977; Scanzoni, 1968; Scanzoni & Szinovaca, 1980; Sprenkle & Olson, 1978).

Recent studies have focused on the decision-making process (Godwin & Scanzoni, 1989; Kingsbury & Scanzoni, 1989). Contextual factors, such as ethnicity, have been acknowledged as being important in understanding how couples make decisions. Strategies, which individuals employ in making decisions, have been identified and related to the resources of individuals. These resources include personality traits and relative wealth, which contribute to decision-making behaviors and outcome.

Our approach to this aspect of relationships was to explore the separate to mutual quality of decision making throughout the three phases of marriage. We focused on a wide range of issues about which couples made decisions, including careers, finances, purchases, leisure, friendships, and child-rearing.

Respondents discussed how they perceived their approach to decisions, which we categorized as logical, impulsive, or intuitive, depending on the predominant way in which they described themselves. Logical decision makers considered the advantages and disadvantages of their choices which were made after a careful consideration of possible outcomes. The impulsive style fell at the other end of the continuum; these individuals acted quickly with little or no thought about their decisions. The intuitive style was defined as a reliance on an inner sense or "gut feeling" rather than on logic or reason. Intuitive decision makers were confident of their innate skills which were not exercised in impulsive ways.

Respondents were also asked to describe how they and their spouses went about making decisions as a couple. These responses were categorized as separate, mutual, or variable (a mixture of separate and mutual).

Sixty-eight percent of all respondents described themselves as logical in their individual approaches to making decisions; 17 percent used words that suggested predominantly impulsive styles; 15 percent said they were highly intuitive about decision making. Individual styles were not significantly different among ethnic or religious groups. Minor but significant differences were found between college and noncollege graduates and between men and women. College graduates reported logical styles more frequently than did other respondents ($p = < .09$). Among the 32 percent of respondents who described nonlogical styles, most wives saw themselves as intuitive and most husbands considered themselves impulsive ($p = < .01$).

There were no significant differences in how husbands and wives described the process of making decisions as couples. Prior to children, approximately one-third of respondents recalled decision making as a mutual process, a third as separate, and another third as variable. Mutuality increased throughout the three phases of marriage. Separateness and variability were related to whether decisions were major, such as the purchase of an automobile, or minor, such as everyday issues in rearing children. Differentiation in making decisions was also related to the talents and skills of spouses, such as budgeting skills. A couple's decision making was influenced significantly by culture: compared with others, Mexican Americans reported more mutuality; Jewish respondents described more separateness in their couple decision-making styles.

In the following pages, we discuss four themes as they emerged from the data: individual decision-making styles, the process of couple decision-making, differentiation in making decisions, and the influence of culture on decision-making styles of couples.

INDIVIDUAL DECISION MAKING

Most respondents identified their decision-making styles as logical. Self-reports of logical decision making remained relatively consistent with 68 percent of respondents describing themselves as logical during the early years of marriage and 72 percent describing themselves that way in the third phase. An example of a logical decision-making style was depicted by Harold, a 56-year-old male married for thirty-seven years:

> I try to consider everything that could go wrong, everything that could go right . . . I try to see the worst case scenario of whatever it could be, and that's the way I look at it, and I attack it from that way. I try to.

As we have already pointed out, individual styles were not differentiated by gender. A 55-year-old woman married for thirty-one years described how she made decisions:

> I tend to think about it, and think about the pro's and con's. I tend to weigh the bad things and then the good things, so if the bad things happen, I am

aware of them. If the good things happen, it is a plus. I do not want to be fooled.

Of the twenty respondents who saw themselves as impulsive decision makers, 70 percent were men. That style was illustrated in the comments of John, a 58-year-old man:

If I have a problem, I want it solved right there ... I feel I am impulsive when it comes to decisions. I just want to get it over with.

Several husbands viewed impulsive styles as part of their personalities which they believed were characteristic of being male:

If I wanted to buy something I just bought it. I just went out and bought it ... if I liked something I would go ahead and buy it. I thought my decision was a good decision. This is the way I was brought up ... the little macho me.

Other husbands associated their styles with male maturity and decisiveness as reflected in the words of Ken, a 54-year-old male:

I was quick to act ... I was quick to make a decision. I would make a decision and do it, and I tended to think it was maturity.

Of the eighteen respondents who described their styles as intuitive, 83 percent were women. A 63-year-old woman, Doreen, married for forty years with five children, was confident about using her intuition to make decisions:

I am sure about a lot of things ... I have good intuitions, then I usually sleep on it.

Some respondents attributed intuition to a higher power. Gloria, married for thirty-four years, described the role of God in her intuitive approach to decisions:

I go to sleep, and when I wake up the Lord has planted different things in my mind. Or I'll say, "Lord, such and such a thing is going to happen. Take it over." It does not always happen the next day. But during the time that it should come due, something will come into my mind to do, to deal with whatever problem I have at the time.

Individual decision-making styles remained constant throughout the three phases of marriage. When both spouses had a systematic and rational approach that characterized logical decision making, conflict about differences was manageable and the stability of relationships was enhanced. Differences between individuals also had a stabilizing effect on marital relationships. The complementary nature of different individual styles was evident in the observations of Edward:

> I just look at things scattered, and that is the way I do things, scattered. It's not right, but I see it getting done ... but my wife sees the more logical path, the more rational way of doing things so I let her do it. Decisions, I always left up to her. I'm lousy at it.

SEPARATENESS TO MUTUALITY IN COUPLE DECISION MAKING

The process of couple decision making was explored by asking whether decisions were made mutually or primarily by one partner throughout the three phases of marriage. Although minimal differences were found in the ways husbands and wives described their decision making, wives talked more of mutuality in couple decision making and husbands of separateness. Two themes emerged from the data: one was the change in separateness and mutuality of decision making from the early years to the empty-nest years; 38 percent remembered couple decision making as primarily separate in phase one which declined to 18 percent in phase three. Between phases one and three, mutuality in decision making increased from 34 percent to 48 percent. Variable decision-making styles of couples remained relatively constant throughout marriage but went up slightly during child-rearing. In the beginning phase, 28 percent of respondents described their decision making as variable; that is, depending on circumstances, it was mutual or separate. During the parenting years variability increased to 36 percent and then declined to 33 percent in the empty-nest years.

For some couples, the process of making decisions was characterized by mutuality throughout marriage. They talked about making decisions jointly. All but the most unimportant decisions were made together. The following couple, both of whom had logical individual styles, described the mutual quality of their approach to decisions throughout thirty-seven years of marriage. Jeff said:

We talked over the situation, tried to analyze the minuses and the pluses, and thought about logical conclusions on which way to go. We share that. It is not her decision or my decision.

Jill, his wife, observed:

We always talked about every important decision, and we usually came to a consensus. Never had a lot of trouble with that.

Among couples who maintained separateness in decision making, some shifts occurred by the third phase even when power was allocated according to traditional gender roles. To maintain balance in their relationships, both spouses had to remain accepting of the reciprocity of their roles, as one husband said:

I don't mean to suggest that she is meek or that I dominate her because I don't think that's true, but I think all of those decisions essentially have been mine because she wants them to be.

His wife of forty-three years agreed with him, although she noted minor changes over the years:

I had nothing to say. That's the way it should be, I think. I like that he is the breadwinner and I am the wife and we talk things over. Now, because of women's lib, I have a lot more to say. In the old days, he told me I had nothing to say about it . . . I respected his opinion.

In some relationships characterized by separateness in decision making, wives had more power than husbands. The reciprocity of their roles was quite different from that of the preceding couple. The following couple illustrates that pattern. The husband acknowledged:

I'm not a decision maker. I don't like to make decisions. So, whenever there is a decision that needs to be made, we get together and talk about it and I'll say, "Whatever you think." If it was up to me, we wouldn't have this house. If it was up to me, we'd be driving a junk; if it was up to me, we'd never have a business.

The reciprocal quality of influence in their relationship was evident in the wife's observations:

There are no differences of opinions, I'm always right. My husband has a hard time making decisions. He puts that responsibility on me and if there is a difference of opinion, we'll sit down and talk about it and I'll give him my views and he'll give his views. I'm always right . . . I think it's very innate. I mean I had that in me. I've always been a decision maker, and I'm always in positions of decision making in my home and jobs . . . the fact that he gives me the freedom makes it easy.

Change from separate to mutual in making decisions was a process that needed to be understood within the context of marriage as a whole. Changes usually happened gradually and, more often than not, were part of other shifts that were occurring in relationships. In several marriages in which power was ascribed to husbands, wives had to be very patient about their expectations for mutuality in decision making. Carol, a 58-year-old woman married for 33 years, commented on the process:

Now we sit down and analyze the whole gamut of possibilities. I know he has made decisions on his own that I disagreed with. In some instances, earlier in the marriage, he made decisions without consulting me that sometimes did not turn out to be the right decision. I made sure I would not say "I told you so" . . . we just grinned and bore it . . . after a while he would say, "I should have listened to you" . . . I think that not antagonizing him helped to improve things and led to more joint decisions.

DIFFERENTIATION IN MAKING DECISIONS

We explored how respondents understood their couple decision-making styles by asking what they thought contributed to mutuality, separateness, and variability. Three themes emerged from the data: the major to minor nature of decisions, circumstances, and the talents and skills of each spouse.

Respondents talked of the separateness to mutuality in making decisions as a product of how "big" or "small" a decision was. That differentiation was reflected in the comments of Maribel, a 52-year-old woman:

Small decisions, each one would be capable of making their own decisions, but buying a car or something big we would confer about it.

Separateness in decision making was associated with circumstances, especially the differences between career and home. A 59-year-old male spoke to that differentiation:

Major decisions were made mutually. There were a lot of decisions that involved my work life that I made independently . . . maybe that was not fair, but I did it.

From the perspective of women respondents who did not work outside the home, separateness was frequently connected with the reality of having primary responsibility for the home and child-rearing. Cora, married for forty-four years with three children, discussed that aspect of decision making:

I always had free reign in terms of the children, needs for the children, and needs for the home.

A third factor that shaped how couples made decisions was related to the differences in the talents and skills of spouses. Respondents talked of being talented in some ways but not in other ways. They referred to skills with budgeting, talent in decorating, and skills in negotiating purchases of items such as automobiles. Differentiation from the viewpoints of a wife and husband is illustrated in the following excerpts. Debra spoke of her role as decision maker:

It wasn't shared. Certain things he didn't care about and left totally to me. On things that we disagreed about, I think most of the time I did it my way.

David, her husband of forty years, agreed and commented on his wife's skill as a planner:

Basically she was the main one to do it, because she loves to plan things and work it out . . . she's a good planner from beginning to end.

Differences in style became a source of stress in relationships in which a spouse's expectations did not fit with that individual's capabilities. In other marriages, spouses were not able to have what they wished and were unable to negotiate a solution to such a dilemma. Eve, a 44-year-old woman married for twenty-three years discussed that dilemma:

One of the things about my marriage that has caused tension is that he won't make a decision . . . I think he's basically very insecure and he's so afraid of making the wrong decision, that he always says, "It's up to you." And I don't want that. I want the husband to be more in control.

CULTURE AND COUPLE DECISION MAKING

Ethnicity and religion influenced the decision-making styles of couples in two ways. Although separateness in couple decision-making styles remained fairly constant throughout marriage for the three ethnic groups, Mexican Americans reported more mutuality in making decisions than did other respondents. Mexican Americans also reported less variability in their decision making as couples. By the empty-nest years, 83 percent of Mexican Americans compared to 40 percent of whites and 39 percent of African Americans described couple decision making as a mutual process [X^2 (4, $N = 120) = 16.87, p = < .01$].

Although the Mexican-American family has been characterized as a patriarchal system (Murillo, 1971; Ybarra, 1978) in which the husband is dominant and the wife submissive in decision making, our findings suggest a far more complex relationship between these husbands and wives. The data are similar to another study of Mexican-American couples (Ybarra, 1978) which reported that 80 percent of couples made joint decisions on large purchases, employment, child-rearing, and the family budget. Seventy-five percent of that sample stated there was equality in their decision making. The process of mutuality is depicted by the following couple who talked of their style of decision making about finances on a limited income. Referring to the challenge of budgeting, Jorge said:

> My wife helped me a lot. She really knows how to budget her money ... we talk about how we're going to do this and that. We don't have no problem at all.

Josephina talked of how she and Jorge went about making decisions:

> I don't think it's been so hard.... You know I say, well this is better, and then sometimes I go around with this idea and then he goes along with it ... you talk about it and sometimes your idea wins out and sometimes his idea wins out. It all depends. We always have talked.... Whenever I plan to do anything, or buy anything, or try to get anything done, I talk to him first. Like, they call me or ask me if you want to have this or that done and I say, well you know I have to talk to my husband. So, we both make decisions.

The process of their decision making contained elements of mutuality and variability as well as respect for the thoughts of each spouse. It also illustrated the quiet yet influential roles that Mexican-American women played in their marriages. Decision making was a complex process and did not fit with the image of marriage dominated by men. In following cultural norms about gender behaviors, several Mexican-American women showed overt respect for their husbands while delicately influencing their decision-making behaviors. This strategy was highlighted by a 56-year-old Mexican woman:

> I solve problems differently than my husband in the sense that I look at the practicality as a woman. . . . My husband would say, "Well, do we really need it?" and "Oh, it can wait." Then I have to go in and help him see, like I said, we women manipulate them. "Well, this will help us with this." Then he says, "You know, I think I'll go ahead and do this." And he thinks it's his own idea, but I would never do a put-down on him. I always make them feel that it's their own idea, not to make him feel they are macho or whatever, but to make them feel that it's their own right, but not that we had to give in. But in the end we get what we want. That always happens ... They realize what's going on, but I think their pride is saved, but yet they realize it was not all them.

In contrast to African Americans and whites, Mexican Americans reported less variability in their decision making, a pattern found over the three phases of marriage. That difference may reflect the significance of family values which prescribed mutuality in decision making in most aspects of marriage. White and African-American couples appeared to be very similar in their decision-making styles, which supports the observation that decision making was shaped less by racial factors and more by other dynamics, such as personality and economic resources.

The other cultural dynamic that yielded significant differences between groups was religion. Even though mutuality in decision making increased for all groups as marriages matured, separateness characterized the decision making of Jewish couples. By the third phase, 37 percent of Jewish respondents compared to 12 percent of Catholics and Protestants talked more of separateness in decision making [$X^2 (4, N = 120) = 10.75, p = .03$]. The theme of separateness among Jewish respondents is illustrated by Arthur and Allison who had been married thirty-three years. Arthur was a businessman, and Allison never worked outside the home. Arthur reported:

> I guess I was really the decision maker. I made any major decisions. She would shy away from them, even though I think I would ask her opinion on things. She seemed to have wanted me to make the decisions, although we've turned that around in later years ... when she grew up, the woman in the house didn't take care of a lot of things ... outside the house; I know in my mother's

case that my dad seemed to make the decision on most everything.... So, I just accepted that role, but as I say, in these latter years, that's really changed a lot.... it's in this later stage when the children are gone that Allison is really making a lot more of the decisions.

In reflecting on her role in this dimension of their marriage, Allison observed:

I think Arthur has always been the problem solver. And I'm more laid back. ... I depend on him, and like oh, this is the problem and I can't think of any problem per se at this moment, but he just has always taken care of me.

The differences between these two people in how they went about making decisions are more pronounced than those in the previous examples of Mexican-American couples. However, the processes of decision making were complex. As with Arthur and Allison, changes occurred as spouses negotiated transitions from one phase of marriage to another. For example, Allison assumed greater responsibility for decision making about financial matters in the post-parenting years. She was ready to take on a different role as was Arthur who was receptive to having his wife take care of matters he had handled for thirty years.

Another aspect of the complexity in decision making was that power and influence were played out at different levels within relationships. Overtly, couples talked frequently of mutuality in making decisions. At the same time, there were covert dynamics that had powerful effects on outcomes. Women often commented on the quiet yet influential roles that they played in shaping the process and outcomes of decision making. Internalization of gender roles that ascribed and then reinforced dominance in men and submissiveness in women shaped the process of decision making. Although most obvious in the interviews with Mexican-American women, these dynamics were present in one form or another in many relationships.

Circumstances interacting with cultural norms had a powerful effect on decision making. In the Jewish sample, the majority of the husbands were businesspersons who worked long hours outside the home. They valued being successful at their careers. Jewish wives defined themselves as the primary caretakers of the home and valued their roles in supporting their husbands' careers. As a consequence, there was often a division between outside work and home work. These couples negotiated a differentiation of roles in which husbands pursued their careers and wives accepted responsibility for decisions about the home and children. A Jewish husband described the separateness of decision-making roles in his marriage:

Let me put it this way, at home she was the boss, in the business I was the boss ... at home whatever my wife wanted as far as running the house I paid the bills. Whatever happens in the house she makes the decisions ... what she wants or doesn't want.

Jewish respondents recalled that the career responsibilities of husbands were more demanding during the child-rearing years when wives made most decisions about the home and children. There was a shift away from individual to a more mutual decision-making style in the years after the children left home. During the post-parenting years roles were defined less clearly. This shift was associated with wives not having the daily care of children and husbands not needing to spend as much time on their careers.

SUMMARY

In observing their own approaches to making decisions, most respondents viewed themselves as individuals who weighed various factors before arriving at decisions. A logical style was a valuable resource when individuals engaged in the process of couple decision making. A minority of respondents used language that suggested an intuitive or impulsive approach to making decisions as individuals. Logical types fitting together in a symmetrical way were no more satisfied with the process of decision making as a couple than were spouses who were very different from each other, such as an impulsive individual married to a systematic thinker.

Separateness, variability, and mutuality were characteristic of couple decision making throughout marriage. In the early years, approximately one out of three respondents' descriptions of their approaches to making decisions as a couple fell into each of these three categories. That pattern did not change appreciably until the empty-nest years. During that phase, variability did not change, but separateness declined and mutuality increased. Mutual decision making then characterized the decision making of almost half the sample, a change reported by all respondents regardless of gender, educational level, religion, or ethnicity. Within that overall trend, differences were found in the decision-making styles of couples depending on cultural factors. Jewish respondents compared with Catholics and Protestants described more separateness in making decisions as a couple. Mexican Americans described more mutuality in the process of making decisions as a couple than did African Americans and whites. Respondents in the latter two groups expressed similar observations about the process of decision making, which suggested that factors in addition to race were influential in couple decision making. The most important finding about decision making was the increase in mutuality as marriages matured.

REFERENCES

Bean, F. D., Curtis, R. L., & Marcum, J. P. (1977). Familism and marital satisfaction among Mexican Americans: The effect of family size, wife's labor force participation, and conjugal power. *Journal of Marriage and the Family, 39*, 759–767.

Bjorksten, O., & Stewart, T. J. (1984). Contemporary trends in American marriages. In C. C. Nadelson & D. C. Polonsky (Eds.), *Marriage and divorce: A contemporary perspective* (pp. 3–60). New York: Guilford Press.

Blood, R. (1969). *Marriage* (Second Edition). New York: The Free Press.

Goodwin, D. & Scanzoni, J. (1989). Couple consensus during marital joint decision-making: A context, process, outcome model. *Journal of Marriage and the Family, 51* (November), 943–956.

Kingsbury, N., & Scanzoni, J. (1989). Process, power and decision outcomes among dual-career couples. *Journal of Comparative Family Studies, XX* (2), 231–246.

Murillo, N. (1971). The Mexican American family. In N. N. Wagner & M. J. Haug (Eds.), *Chicanos: Social and psychological perspectives* (pp. 97–108). St. Louis: C. V. Mosby Co.

Prochaska, J., & Prochaska, J. (1978). Twentieth century trends in marriage and marital therapy. In T. Paolino and B. McCrady (Eds.), *Marriage and marital therapy.* New York: Brunner/Mazel.

Reibstein, J. (1988). Family therapy and sex role development throughout the life-cycle: A useful concept. *Journal of Family Therapy, 10*, 153–166.

Scanzoni, J. (1968). A social system analysis of dissolved and existing marriages. *Journal of Marriage and the Family, 30*, 452–461.

Scanzoni, J., & Szinovaca, M. (1980). *Family decision-making.* Beverly Hills, Calif.: Sage Publications.

Sprenkle, D. H., & Olson, D. H. (1978). Circumplex model of marital systems: An empirical study of clinic and nonclinic couples. *Journal of Marriage and Family Counseling, 4*, 59–74.

White, L. K. (1990). Determinants of divorce: A review of research in the eighties. *Journal of Marriage and the Family, 52*, 904–912.

Ybarra, L. (1978). Marital decision-making and the role of machismo in the Chicano family. *De Colores Journal, 6*, 32–47.

—6—

Parenting

... if love had been money, they'd be millionaires today ... I adored
my kids ... they were my life ...

Marriages became more complex as spouses added the roles of parenting
to their relationships. Integrating these new roles into their relationships
was a challenge for couples no matter how well prepared and ready they
were to take on the responsibilities of rearing children. In the interests of
child-rearing, intimacy was sometimes compromised. The needs of children
at different stages of development led to conflict between spouses about
appropriate parental responses. Responsibilities for the socialization of
children caused stress for additional reasons, not the least of which was that
child-rearing was often paradoxical: parents needed to be empathic, supportive, and understanding of their children; at the same time, they had to
set limits, maintain boundaries, and control their children. These were not
easy skills to integrate into the role of being a parent.

In this study, the parenting phase was defined as the years between the
birth of the first child and the eighteenth birthday of the youngest child. The
significance of child-rearing to marital relationships was explored in rela-

tion to infancy, childhood, and adolescence. We explored how husbands and wives adapted to the challenges of becoming mothers and fathers: How were these new roles integrated into their marital relationships? How did spouses negotiate tasks of nurturing and disciplining children? Were the responsibilities of child-rearing differentiated by gender or were they shared by spouses? Did those responsibilities change throughout the second phase of marriage? What impact did children have on the quality of marital relationships?

Several studies have examined the effects on marriage of the transition into parenthood. In their review of eleven studies, Cowan et al. (1985) found only one in which marital satisfaction increased in the months following the birth of the first child. In nine of the studies, there was a decline in marital satisfaction up to nine months after birth. In a longitudinal study of seventy-two couples who were followed from the last trimester of pregnancy to the ninth postpartum month (Belsky, Spanier, & Rovine,1983), "modest" negative changes were reported in marital relationships. Adverse effects were more evident on wives rather than husbands and among couples with more than one child. Lewis (1988) differentiated levels of marital quality prior to birth and then at three months and one year postpartum. His data suggested that the quality of marriages prior to children played an important role in understanding marital relationships after the arrival of children. Highly cohesive and close marriages prior to children were the most stable during the first postpartum year. Couples whose marriages were highly conflictual prior to the birth of a child appeared to be most vulnerable to deterioration in their relationships.

Research examining the quality of marriage across the family life cycle has hypothesized a "curvilinear" or "U-shaped" pattern in marital relationships from early marriage through the child-rearing years and into the empty-nest phase (Rollins & Cannon, 1974; Rollins & Feldman, 1970). Several studies have found that marital quality is high in the early years, declines during child-rearing, and returns to a high-quality level in the empty-nest phase. That hypothesis was accepted widely until challenged by Spanier, Lewis, and Cole (1975) who used a standardized measure of marital adjustment on a sample of 1,574 couples from three states. Their findings offered only partial support for curvilinearity. Adjustment at different phases of marriage varied by geographic region: couples from Iowa reported minimal regression during child-rearing, while those from Ohio reported the most regression; by the third phase, marital adjustment was on the rise for all couples.

Most studies of change in marriage across the family life cycle have used retrospective or cross-sectional designs rather than longitudinal methodologies which Spanier et al. (1975) recommended. In a longitudinal study of male Harvard graduates, which also included their wives, the Vaillants (1993) had the unusual opportunity to use both retrospective and prospective measures in assessing marital quality. Retrospectively, the findings confirmed the curvilinear hypothesis; a U-shaped pattern in relationships was found, with marital quality reaching a low level during the child-rearing years and rebounding in the later years. Wives felt that the most difficult times for their marriages were during the children's adolescence. When comparable measures of marital quality (overall satisfaction, problem solving, and sexual enjoyment) which had been made prospectively at specific points throughout these marriages were examined, curvilinearity was not as apparent. That is, retrospective measures yielded more support for the curvilinear hypothesis than did prospective measures.

Given the questions raised by previous studies, especially those of Lewis (1988), Spanier et al. (1975), and the Vaillants (1993), we explored how respondents in our study experienced the effects of child-rearing on their marriages. We have already discussed how these marriages changed: instrumental and expressive roles that had been differentiated by gender early in marriage became more integrated during the parenting phase, although husbands continued to identify themselves primarily in instrumental terms; conflict, often about the rearing of children, became more serious during the second phase of marriage; wives more than husbands reported feelings of inequity about the allocation of tasks and responsibilities; sexual relations became less frequent; and satisfaction with sex declined, more so for wives than for husbands. The question of curvilinearity was important in itself but was more intriguing since the respondents in our study represented greater cultural diversity than respondents in other studies.

Before examining parenting and its effect on marriage, it is important to clarify some characteristics of these families. Although no significant differences were found by ethnicity, whites were more likely to have one or two children, African Americans three or four, and Mexican Americans five or more. Catholics compared with Protestants and Jews had larger families. Seventy-three percent of couples with five or more children were Catholic. Conversely, 76 percent of Protestant and Jewish couples had one or two children [X^2 (4, $N = 120$) $= 17.26$, $p = < .001$]. The higher the level of education, the lower the number of children: 52 percent of respondents with a college education had one or two children compared with 26 percent of respondents with less than a college education; of those with five or more children, 18 percent were college graduates [X^2 (2, $N = 120$) = 9.34, $p = < .01$].

INFANCY AND CHILDHOOD

We were interested in how the roles of caring for children from infancy through adolescence were allocated within marital relationships. Respondents were asked for their perceptions of who was responsible for child-rearing during infancy, childhood, and adolescence. Responses to that question fell along a continuum: those who described responsibilities as separate or individual clustered toward one pole, and those who described responsibilities as mutual or joint clustered toward the other pole.

Seventy-one percent of respondents reported that mothers did most, if not all, of the caring of infants; 29 percent of respondents remembered the caring of infants as a mutual responsibility of both mothers and fathers. As children grew, fathers became progressively involved in parenting. By latency, 46 percent of respondents talked of parenting as a mutual responsibility, a 17 percent increase from the infancy subphase. There was a close correspondence in the reports of husbands and wives; no significant differences were found by gender. In addition, little variation in this pattern was found by educational level or religion. The only significant difference was found among African Americans, more of whom talked of parenting as a mutual responsibility during infancy [X^2 (2, $N = 120$) = 8.27, $p = .02$]; that difference, albeit weaker, continued through adolescence ($p = < .08$).

During infancy, separateness in parenting roles was described by the following couple, the parents of four children. Their response was illustrative of the overall pattern of parenting roles, although the specific nature of how couples worked out parenting responsibilities varied. Mike, a 70-year-old retired blue-collar worker recalled:

As far as taking care of the kids, I think poor Mary did 90 percent of the work. Washed the babies, fed them, changed the diapers . . . I don't think I changed half a dozen diapers in my life. That was all my wife . . . She worked hard.

His 65-year-old spouse, Mary, commented:

He says to me: "You really took over the whole responsibility of the children"; I did. . . . He was very, very busy . . . they had to answer to me . . . I was the big bad wolf. And there was no problem. They all did very well. He provided, and provided well. He was very good to the children, I mean, he'd almost sacrifice himself . . . what he wanted for them was more or less what I expected of them.

For this couple and others, allocation of parenting roles was shaped substantially by economic factors. Even among college graduates who earned higher salaries, however, mothers were primarily responsible for nurturing infants and caring for children. In fact, the separateness in parenting roles was slightly higher among college graduates than it was among respondents with less than a college education. The cultural mores of the time ascribed the role of provider to husbands and nurturer to wives. Clearly, cultural dynamics were more powerful than economic ones in molding the roles of spouses as they became mothers and fathers.

Parenting roles were not as clearly differentiated as the categories of separate and mutual suggest. The boundary between the two categories was not demarcated precisely, although the predominant responsibilities for nurturing, caregiving, and discipline were clear enough for our purposes. Fathers usually assumed the roles of helper or backup to mothers. The following couple, both college graduates, described how they worked out complementary roles in parenting their two children. The father commented:

> I think I have been a good father. It is not like it is today. When our children were born, I took my wife to the hospital and was ushered out the door. You weren't supposed to be part of the process. I think that has all changed. I think there is more of a nurturing role within a relationship than before. I was not involved in the diaper changing. I have a very weak stomach. She took care of the kids, but I would baby-sit when she had things to do.

His wife observed:

> He probably only changed five diapers in his whole life. I was responsible for the child care. He was always great about babysitting if I wanted to do some volunteer work or if I wanted to do something special. He was always very supportive of my activities. He was wonderful about taking care of the kids and enjoyed them. I don't think he knew what to do with babies. He certainly did not take the active child care role as most young fathers do nowadays. He would have if that had been expected of him. It did not really occur to us. I was at home, he was at work. He took an active interest in the kids, but not for their care.... The bad balance is being so totally consumed with kids that you don't have time for each other. That's a mistake a lot of people make. We have made an effort not to let that happen. We had to work at that. You can really get sucked into putting your kids first. You can't always do that.

As this woman knew, so much of their behavior as parents was shaped and reinforced by prevailing social expectations of gender roles. Women assumed the nurturing role of mothers; men were available to help them carry out these responsibilities. Given a different context, their parental roles may have evolved differently. What was equally apparent in the observations of this woman was an awareness of balancing child-caring responsibilities with attention to the marriage. Many women talked of the importance of attending to their husbands along with caring for children, which may have helped to neutralize conflict during the child-rearing years.

By the latency years of children, 46 percent of the husbands were actively involved in parenting. Although mothers had the primary responsibility for taking care of children, there was a quality of mutuality in parenting roles. For example, listen to the themes in the memories of the parents of four children.

He reported:

> I wasn't certainly a prima donna. I'd be happy to give her a time, but when we had most of the child-rearing I was an apprentice and I didn't have much time to do anything ... I wouldn't hesitate but she wouldn't think to ask you to change the diaper, not that I didn't do it when she wasn't there but when she was there she felt it was her job. Not that I felt that it was, because lots of things I've always helped with ... the children ... I was always there if needed. If something had to be corrected it was done there by whoever. And there was no criticism on her part or my part over discipline. I guess we have the same values.

She offered the following observations:

> He was very helpful. I have to laugh today that the men need this bonding with the children. Any man I knew ... were [sic] always very involved with their children, involved with the house ... The world has changed that much I know. But at the time, he was very helpful. Every Saturday I'd go shopping and he'd take care of these four children. And I'd leave in the morning ... and eat my lunch ... and shop around just for the day. He was very helpful and a wonderful father. I couldn't say that he wasn't, but every other man I knew was too.

ADOLESCENCE

Adolescence is a turning point for children, a developmental transition from childhood to adulthood. It is also a transition for parents who are confronted with a different developmental agenda in their children and with an impending change in their relationships: they will soon be alone again. The quality of marital relationships will determine how couples will adapt to those changes. Numerous studies have been done on this stage of the family life cycle (Offer & Schonert-Reichl,1992; Silverberg & Steinberg, 1987; Steinberg, 1987; Youniss & Ketterlinus, 1987). As children negotiate their way through adolescence, parents may be facing their own midlife transitions. The relationship between these two developmental dynamics has been studied by Koski and Steinberg (1990) who found that a satisfying marriage may help to neutralize the stresses associated with parenting adolesents while contending with one's midlife issues.

Among the three subphases of parenting, adolescence produced the most stress on marital relationships. Conflict increased significantly, and satisfaction with marriage declined for both spouses, especially among women; 50 percent of women felt dissatisfied with their marriages during the parenting years, and their satisfaction reached its lowest point during the adolescent subphase.

The trend among husbands to become involved in parenting continued through childhood and into adolescence. By the third subphase, 57 percent of respondents talked of parenting as a mutual responsibility. That was almost double the rate of mutuality reported when children were infants. A variation on that theme was found among Jewish couples. During the adolesent subphase, responsibility for parenting was described as separate by 63 percent of Jewish respondents compared to 42 percent of Catholics and 30 percent of Protestants [X^2 (2, $N = 120$) = 7.82, $p = .02$]. Twenty percent of Jewish wives who did not work outside the home retained primary responsibility for parenting. Even among those who were employed outside the home, parenting continued to be the prime responsibility of Jewish wives.

There were two reasons for the increased involvement of fathers in child-rearing. One was economic. As women became employed outside of the home, often to earn enough money to send their children to college or to resume careers, couples negotiated new arrangements for child-rearing. These changes led to greater mutuality in caring for and disciplining children. The second reason for the husbands' increased involvement in parenting was family conflict triggered by adolescent development.

Carlos, a Mexican-American father of two daughters, expressed a theme evident in the responses of many parents as they coped with losing their children to adulthood:

I like my girls to be here; I wish I could keep them here all the time, but they are ... grown up and everything.... I guess I sort of got attached to them when they were little and I had them here all the time, and now they're growing up and each of them are on their way going to different places. So, it's awfully hard to get adjusted to being lonely. Back then, of course, there was a lot of screaming and this and that you know, and now it's kind of different. But I love my kids and I love my wife, and over the years there are a lot of adjustments to be made.

Cenci, his wife, talked of her beliefs about discipline which were different from her husband's. These differences became more problematic as their daughters negotiated adolescence:

He had in mind that you're supposed to hit them or slap them, and I didn't believe in that. I thought of punishment like they wouldn't be allowed to go any place for the next week or two. That was my kind of punishment, and if he wanted to hit them I always got in between.... But he really wasn't that bad ... sometimes he did it to scare them. But he was an easy, down to earth father and he understood most of the stuff, but I think that was when we got into arguments, that was the difference, that I didn't like them being hit.

A common source of tension between teenagers and parents was setting limits and maintaining reasonable boundaries. Repeatedly, that theme came up in the stories of respondents as with these middle-class parents of three children. The husband commented:

How do you allow a teenager to live in your home and make a mess out of her room and tell your wife to shut the door because it's her room and "not your room?" ... if she wants to be a slob, she is gonna be.... When my son grew his hair down to his shoulders, I said: "Thank God if that is all he is gonna do." ... We did not think we were gonna survive the teen years. One morning our daughter did not come in until three in the morning. I went upstairs; we got into bed. My wife said: "You can't go to sleep, your daughter's not home." I said: "Well, there are only two things that could be happening. She is either staying overnight somewhere or she has been killed. It is either too late and she has decided not to call and wake us up, or she is gonna call. Sitting up worrying is not gonna do any good." I went to sleep. She hammered me on the back and said that I was insensitive to her needs.

Along with stress which generally accompanies the transition of adolescence into early adulthood, spouses described how they worked together to cope with change. The wife in the above marriage remembered her husband as

> Good with the kids.... If problems arose, we would discuss them. We tried not to disagree about raising the kids in front of them which is easier said than done. Generally speaking, I would say that we were able to achieve that. We battled things out behind closed doors. We had to give them a consistency in the manner of how we were gonna raise them. Neither one of us have ever been afraid to say when we were wrong to our kids. I feel very proud about that. We all make mistakes. Child-rearing is the biggest job we do, and we only have one shot at it. We learn a lot from our mistakes. We don't always do it right. If you can swallow your pride and say, "OK, I blew it, I realize I should not have been so hard on you," the kids have a lot more respect for you. We have never been afraid to say that we were wrong when we were wrong.

Being honest and straightforward with children was valued by respondents. Many, including this mother, thought that it was important to maintain a united front with adolescents and to resolve differences with their husbands about child-rearing in private. The data suggest that the adolescent years represented an important transition in marriages as these middle-aged parents helped their children to negotiate separation/individuation. Mutuality in parenting helped to pave the road to enhanced intimacy and satisfaction between spouses after their children left home.

PARENTING AND ETHNICITY

Ethnicity had a significant effect on parenting in two ways:

1. Compared with others, African-American respondents talked of parenting as a mutual responsibility of both spouses, a difference that was found throughout the three sub-phases; and
2. The extended family of the spouse being interviewed in Mexican-American marriages was viewed as having a very positive influence during the parenting years.

Fifty percent of African Americans viewed the care and nurturing of infants as a mutual responsibility, compared to 25 percent of whites and 18 percent of Mexican Americans [X^2 (2, $N = 120$) = 8.27, $p = .02$]. As we have already observed, there was a steady increase in mutuality for all groups through the childhood years. By adolescence, mutual responsibility for parenting had increased to 50 percent for Mexican Americans, 52 percent for whites, and 75 percent for African Americans.

These data challenge stereotypes about African-American families which have been viewed as matriarchal. Research over the past thirty years focusing on the dynamics of power and decision making among black couples has found variability in the power structure of their marital relationships (Gray-Little, 1982; Middleton & Putney, 1960; TenHouten, 1970; Willie, 1976). Similar to marriages in general, African-American marriages vary more by social class status than by race (Mack, 1978; TenHouten, 1970; Willie & Greenblatt, 1978). Our findings about mutuality in child-rearing among African-American couples spoke to the dynamics of power in these marriages. Fathers spoke assertively about the importance of their roles in rearing children. The theme of equity in parenting was expressed by Felix, a father of four children who was now in his seventies:

> Fay did more disciplining . . . because I was working. But when I came home, I would do my part . . . it was always about the same with us. Both of us shared the responsibilities for the children 50–50.

Fay confirmed the mutuality in their roles as parents:

> We didn't have no problem with our kids. When the kids came along, I never got up with the kids at night. I took care of 'em all day, got 'em ready for bed and everything, but if they woke up in the night, he always got up with them. So we worked together with the kids. We didn't have no problems. . . . Felix and I used to take time to teach them. They knew how to dial the phone when they were a little over a year old . . . both of us tried to teach them.

Mutuality among African-American parents was manifested in various ways. The following couple, the parents of five children, worked out child-rearing roles somewhat differently from Felix and Fay. Mutuality for them was based on dividing tasks. Harold said:

> We worked together. During the day she would take care of them. And during the nights, when I came home, I would chip in . . . I would help feed and take care of them at night, let her get some rest. That's how we did it basically with all our children . . . we had to work together a lot, lot more, say, from the first two. But we used to split up the duties. I would help cook . . . we set up a schedule on how we're going to do things. And that's basically how we got through that period. . . . When they got older, she used to take them to school, you know . . . she went off to work at 2:30 in the afternoon . . . I would come home . . . I'd finish up the supper and help them with their homework.

And I would get them ready for bed. And that's the way it went from day to day ... we worked together ... and it worked out pretty good ... she did most of the disciplining. But whatever she did, I did back it up. I would have to back it up or it wouldn't be any good. But that was basically her department. And it still is.

Heidi remembered how they worked out child-rearing. Although she introduced some new data about disciplining the children, the theme of mutuality remained consistent:

When we had our children I wasn't working, I was a housewife. And I was the one that took care of them mostly, making sure they did their homework and went to school. If they were sick, I'd take care of them ... when he would get home from work he would take over, you know, and give me a little rest in between. He would take care of them up until 12:00 at night, with whatever small one might wake up at night. So we did share as far as taking care of the kids and everything ... with the two boys, he always kept them very active, because he was nuts about sports and everything ... but ... I did disciplining ... he was a softy. He always threatened he was going to do that, but I really did.

In addition to culturally shaped values about the importance of sharing child-rearing responsibilities, two other factors reinforced mutuality among African-American couples. First, as children grew, mothers returned to work to contribute to the financial security of families, and, as with other blue-collar respondents who were not college graduates, they wanted a better life for their children. One way of achieving that goal was to have enough money to send their children to college. A second factor was related to the cutoff of these families from their kin. Most African Americans had moved away from their extended families; as a consequence, spouses relied on each other for support. In contrast to Mexican Americans and whites most of whom lived close to their extended families, 60 percent of African Americans reported that their extended families had no influence on them in the child-rearing years.

The extended families of Mexican Americans had a highly positive influence on them throughout marriage. In relation to rearing children, 63 percent of Mexican-American respondents described their extended families in positive ways compared to 40 percent of white and 21 percent of African-American respondents [X^2 (4, $N = 120$) $= 14.87$, $p = < .01$]. A Mexican-American mother expressed how her mother was an important part of the family during the child-rearing years:

> It was three people who raised my son ... myself, my husband and my mother
> ... I'd say all throughout until he was about 12 or 13. ... We moved over
> here. At the time my son was a baby, my father passed away and shortly
> thereafter, we bought a house to be close to my mother just a block away.

Studies have suggested more geographical clustering and intergenerational cohesiveness among Mexican Americans compared to Anglos (Falicov, 1982; Keefe, 1984; Murillo, 1971; Vega, 1990; Williams, 1990). Taylor
et al. (1990) found that intergenerational relations offered support to a
couple and helped to alleviate marital stress. The extended family, as a
support network in parenting, appeared to enhance the psychological well-
being of dual-earner parents (Holtzman & Gilbert, 1987). Those findings
were important in understanding the meaning of extended families in our
study, since all Mexican-American mothers and fathers were employed
outside the home. Most of these couples had several children, so the
availability of others, notably grandparents, was an important source of
support. Although extended family households appear to be on the decline
(Keefe, 1984), kin networks among Mexican Americans continued to play
a vital role in promoting family solidarity and cohesiveness. Our data
support that hypothesis.

A NOTE ON THE U-SHAPED CURVE

At the beginning of this chapter, we referred to the work of Spanier,
Lewis, and Cole (1975) as well as that of the Vaillants (1993). Both studies
raised serious questions about the validity of the curvilinear hypothesis.
Spanier et al. (1975) concluded that "the question of curvilinearity (was)
not yet settled" (p. 271). They suggested that any U-shaped curve in the
marital life cycle was very complex. The phenomenon of regression during
the parenting years may reflect measurements of some aspect(s) of marital
relationships while ignoring others. Our data suggested that, while regression occurred in some dimensions of marriage, there was progression in
other dimensions. The process was neither unidimensional nor unidirec-
tional.

In assessing the differences in their retrospective and prospective data
on marital satisfaction, the Vaillants (1993) concluded that "the U-curve of
marital satisfaction may be an artifact of retrospective and cross-sectional
study" (p. 238). Prospective measures did not produce the same patterns of
regression as did retrospective measures on which both spouses reported a

U-curve of satisfaction with their relationships. We wonder whether retrospective data may not be more valid about the quality of marriage over time than data collected at planned intervals. Distance may give one a perspective on reality which closeness obscures. That phenomenon may be as true of marriage as it is of certain developmental periods, such as adolescence. As one views reality from afar, the perception of what was happening during that phase of marriage may be more accurate than comparable measures taken when one is immersed in the phase itself. In addition, distance allows one to evaluate that period of time within the context of other phases. Thus, distance may enhance the accuracy of personal evaluation by placing memories into both an historical and a relative context. In looking back, the child-rearing years may not appear as satisfying as the early years before children or the years after the children have matured.

Several changes occurred in marital relationships during the child-rearing phase. On the regressive side, serious conflict increased and was usually focused on differences about the care and discipline of children, especially in adolescence. Sexual relations were not as frequent or as satisfying during the child-rearing years, another change in a regressive direction. A third aspect of relationships which continued to be problematic was that of handling differences in which men continued to be avoidant about dealing with conflict. Finally, half of women respondents recalled prevailing feelings of dissatisfaction with their marriages during the child-rearing years compared to the early years when 63 percent remembered being satisfied.

On the progressive side, an increase in mutuality between spouses was reported, particularly in decision making and child-rearing. In relation to child-rearing, there was a steady growth in husbands becoming more involved in child-rearing from infancy to adolescence. Other aspects of relationships remained fairly constant from the early years of marriages through the child-rearing years. These included the quality of communication, sense of fairness about marriage, as well as relationship variables such as trust, respect, understanding, and sensitivity.

Our findings suggest that there is a "U" type pattern to some aspects of relationships during the second phase of marriage. At the same time, specific qualities that nurture the viability of a relationship remain constant. They provide a balance to the regressive aspects. In a sense, relational qualities such as trust and respect may enable people to tolerate stressful times, as during the adolescence of their children. Although wives became more dissatisfied with marriage during the parenting phase, they reported feeling that the marriage was equitable, that life with the spouse balanced out when one considered all aspects of the relationship. Perhaps the progressive involvement of husbands in child-rearing, which led to a sense of mutuality about being parents, helped to cultivate feelings of fairness. Although sexual intercourse declined, psychological intimacy, which included the openness of communication, remained relatively constant.

Marriage is part of the process of adult development. During certain developmental phases, dimensions of relationships may not go well. Regression may result. At the same time, different dimensions may remain constant, and other aspects may actually progress. The concept of curvilinearity poses questions as to which aspects of marriage regress during child-rearing, which remain constant, and which progress. The information gathered in this study provides some answers to these questions. The data demonstrate that the balance of these dynamics along with other factors, such as external support systems, shapes the quality of marital relationships.

SUMMARY

The second phase of marriage, parenting, began with the birth of the first child and ended with the eighteenth birthday of the youngest child. Our interest was in how parenting roles affected the quality of marital relationships. The separateness to mutuality of child-rearing responsibilities was explored for the infant, latency, and adolescent periods of children's development. Seventy-one percent of mothers had the responsibility for taking care of children during infancy and the early years of childhood. As children grew into latency, fathers became increasingly involved in child-rearing. By that time, 46 percent of fathers were active participants in parenting their children. By the adolescent years, that figure had risen to 57 percent. These findings suggest a progressive shift from separateness to mutuality in parenting responsibilities as children matured. The only significant variation on this theme was among African-American couples. From infancy through adolescence, African-American couples reported higher levels of mutuality in child-rearing compared with Mexican Americans and whites. Among Mexican Americans, the extended family had a more active and positive role in parenting than did other ethnic groups.

The data add to an understanding of the U-shaped curve reported by others in studies of the family life cycle. While some aspects of marital relationships appeared to regress during the parenting phase, other aspects progressed. Overall satisfaction with relationships declined, more among women than men, as did the frequency of sexual intercourse and the importance of sex. Interpersonal conflict between spouses also increased and was often related to differences in child-rearing especially during the adolescent years. At the same time, a sense of mutuality and equity between spouses emerged as they adapted to the needs of a growing family. The positive, or what we referred to as progressive, changes appeared to offer a balance to the natural stresses of raising a family and helped to neutralize regressive changes. These positive shifts in relationships acted as resources for couples to adapt to a life together once the children had grown.

REFERENCES

Belsky, J., Spanier, G. B., & Rovine, M. (1983). Stability and change in marriage across the transition to parenthood. *Journal of Marriage and the Family, 45,* 567–577.

Cowan, C. P., Cowan, P. A., Heming, G., Garrett, E., Coysh, W. S., Curtis-Boles, H., & Boles, A. J., III (1985). Transitions to parenthood: His, hers, and theirs. *Journal of Family Issues, 6* (4), 451–481.

Falicov, C. J. (1982). Mexican families. In M. McGoldrick, J. K. Pearce, & J. Giordant (Eds.), *Ethnicity and family therapy.* New York: Guilford Press.

Gray-Little, B. (1982). Marital quality and power processes among black couples. *Journal of Marriage and the Family, 44,* 633–646.

Holtzman, E. H. & Gilbert, L. A. (1987). Social support networks for parenting and psychological well being among dual-career Mexican American families. *Journal of Community Psychology, 15,* 176–185.

Keefe, S. E. (1984). Acculturation and the extended family among urban Mexican Americans. In A. M. Padilla (Ed.), *Acculturation: Theory models, and some new findings* (pp. 85–110). Boulder, CO: Westview Press.

Koski, K. J., & Steinberg, L. (1990). Parenting satisfaction of mothers during midlife. *Journal of Youth and Adolescence, 19* (5), 25–38.

Lewis, J. M. (1988). The transition to parenthood: II. Stability and change in marital structure. *Family Process, 27,* 273–283.

Mack, D. (1978). The power relationship in black families and white families. In R. Staples (Ed.), *The black American reference book.* Englewood Cliffs, NJ: Prentice-Hall.

Middleton, R., & Putney, S. (1960). Dominance in decisions in the family: Race and class differences. In C. V. Willie (Ed.), *The family life of black people* (pp. 16–22). Columbus, OH: Charles E. Merrill.

Murillo, N. (1971). The Mexican American family. In N. N. Wagner & M. J. Haug (Eds.), *Chicanos: Social and psychological perspectives* (pp. 97–108). St. Louis: C. V. Mosby Co.

Offer, D., & Schonert-Reichl, K. L. (1992). Debunking the myths of adolescence: Findings from recent research. *Journal of the American Academy of Child and Adolescent Psychiatry, 31,* (6), 1003–1014.

Rollins, B. C., & Cannon, K. L. (1974). Marital satisfaction over the family life cycle: A reevaluation. *Journal of Marriage and the Family, 36,* 271–282.

Rollins, B. C., & Feldman, H. (1970). Marital satisfaction over the family life cycle. *Journal of Marriage and the Family, 32,* 20–27.

Silverberg, S. B., & Steinberg, L. (1987). Adolescent autonomy, parent-adolescent conflict and parental well-being. *Journal of Youth and Adolescence, 16,*(3), 293–312.

Spanier, G. B., Lewis, R. A., & Cole, C. L. (1975). Marital adjustment over the family life cycle: The issue of curvilinearity. *Journal of Marriage and the Family, 37,* 263–275.

Steinberg, L. (1987). Family processes at adolescence: A developmental perspective. *Family Therapy, 14,* (2), 77–85.

Taylor, R. J., Chatters, L. R., Tucker, M. B., & Lewis, E. (1990). Developments in research on black families: A decade review. *Journal of Marriage and the Family, 52,* 993–1014.

TenHouten, W. (1970). The black family: Myth and reality. *Psychiatry, 2,* 145–153.

Vaillant, C. O. & Vaillant, G. E. (1993). Is the U-curve of marital satisfaction an illusion? A 40-year study of marriage. *Journal of Marriage and the Family, 55,* 230–239.

Vega, W. A. (1990). Hispanic families in the 1980's: A decade of research. *Journal of Marriage and the Family, 52,* 1015–1024.

Williams, N. (1990). *The Mexican American family: Tradition and change.* Dix Hills, NY: General Hall, Inc.

Willie, C. V. (1976). *A new look at black families.* Bayside, N.Y.: General Hall.

Willie, C. V., & Greenblatt, S. L. (1978). Four classic studies of power relationships in black families. *Journal of Marriage and the Family, 40,* 691–696.

Youniss, J., & Ketterlinus, R. D. (1987). Communication and connectedness in mother and father adolescent relationships. *Journal of Youth and Adolescence, 16* (3), 265–280.

—7—

Marital Satisfaction

It's gotten better . . . the understanding has increased . . . .There is a
flow and I don't know that I can say what all the things are that make
it better . . .

This book, which began with an exploration of how spouses initially were
attracted to each other, ends with how they felt about their lives together
after more than twenty years of marriage. The level of satisfaction, based
on the thoughts and feelings of respondents as they discussed the quality
and meaning of their relationships, was gleaned from responses to several
questions, which included: how relationships had changed or not changed
over the three phases of marriage, commitment to the marriage, containment
of conflict, the sense of intimacy with the spouse, couple decision making,
problem solving, and fairness. Similar to several other variables in this
study, satisfaction was conceptualized along a continuum with positive
responses toward one pole and negative ones toward the other pole. Although satisfaction was evaluated for each phase of marriage, those aspects
of marital relationships which contributed significantly to satisfaction
during the empty-nest years are explored in this chapter. They were:

Containment of conflict

Mutuality in decision making

Quality of communication

Relational values of trust, respect, empathic understanding, and equity

Sexual and psychological intimacy

Before discussing how these factors enhanced satisfaction, themes from contemporary research pertinent to the focus of this chapter will be reviewed. We will then comment on those aspects of marriage which were not related significantly to satisfaction in our study, some of which differed from findings in other studies.

There has been considerable research on understanding marital satisfaction (Aida & Falbo, 1991; Allen & Thompson, 1984; Argyle & Furnham, 1983; Broderick & O'Leary, 1986; Fowers, 1991; Kelley & Burgoon, 1991; Shachar, 1991). Of special interest are studies that explored the potential connection of satisfaction with stability or intactness of marital relationships (Hicks & Platt, 1970; Kelly & Conley, 1987; Lewis & Spanier, 1979; Spanier & Lewis, 1980). There is an inherent connection between being satisfied and staying in a relationship, although the exact nature of that relationship is unknown. Even though many marriages remain intact because spouses are satisfied with their relationships (Lewis & Spanier, 1979), other relationships may endure despite dissatisfaction (Lewis & Spanier, 1979; Spanier & Lewis, 1980). A major difficulty in understanding satisfaction and its relationship to stability results from an inconsistency in defining what constitutes satisfaction. Studies point to the subjective, relative, and variable nature of such a psychosocial state. No matter how well standardized, research instruments are limited in assessing marital satisfaction.

In recent years, there has been increasing research on satisfaction in long-term marriages (Gottman & Krokoff, 1989; Haefner, Notarius, & Pellegrini, 1991; Kelly & Conley, 1987; Lauer, Lauer & Kerr, 1990; Levenson, Carstensen, & Gottman, 1993; Vaillant & Vaillant, 1993). Investigators have studied satisfaction from several perspectives, including antecedent personality dynamics, interpersonal dynamics which evolve within marital relationships, and contextual factors, such as family income. These studies suggest that a state of satisfaction results from the interaction of numerous variables that are not independent of each other.

Data on couples followed since the 1930s in the Kelly longitudinal study indicated that factors antecedent to marriage, such as the level of "neuroticism" within each spouse and the impulsivity of husbands, were the strongest predictors of the quality of marital relationships several decades later (Kelly & Conley, 1987). Neuroticism and impulsivity, which have also been identified in other longitudinal studies, characterized divorced couples as well as couples who remained together in dissatisfied relationships. Studies of marital relationships as they evolve over time add another dimension to understanding satisfaction. In a survey of one hundred middle-class couples who had been married at least forty-five years, friendship with a person whom one liked was identified by respondents as the most important component of satisfaction. Commitment to the marriage as an institution and to the spouse, as well as mutuality of views on various issues, were perceived as important in nurturing satisfaction (Lauer, Lauer & Kerr 1990). Ways in which spouses deal with conflict and resolve problems had an effect not only on physical and psychological well-being, but also on marital satisfaction. Longitudinal studies of couples married more than twenty years have found that couples who employ avoidant defenses to deal with marital conflicts are less satisfied than those who confront conflict (Gottman & Krokoff, 1989). Other research suggests that chronic inability to resolve disagreements erodes marital stability and satisfaction, the consequences of which lead to more psychological and physical impairments among wives than husbands (Levenson, Carstensen, and Gottman, 1993). As part of a longitudinal study of well-educated and affluent Harvard graduates, the Vaillants found a decrease in marital satisfaction among couples married over thirty years (Vaillant & Vaillant, 1993). Wives were somewhat more unhappy than husbands in assessing the success of couples at solving disagreements. Both spouses also reported a decline in sexual satisfaction.

Our approach to understanding satisfaction builds on and complements other efforts in studying this phenomenon. We used a methodology that tapped the underlying meanings associated with being satisfied rather than using standardized measuring instruments. Focal questions elicited data from the perspectives of individual respondents; we did not ask them to fill out questionnaires or complete inventories of marital adjustment scales. Both approaches are useful in building an understanding of the nature of satisfaction, how it is related to stability, and what contributes to it. Another way in which our work builds on other research is in the social diversity of the sample, 43 percent of whom were African Americans and Mexican Americans. Sixty-five percent of respondents represented blue-collar, working people, and there was also diversity in the religious backgrounds of respondents.

Analysis of satisfaction in the post-parenting years revealed several interesting patterns. There was no significant relationship between relational fit and satisfaction. Whether respondents viewed themselves on the same symmetrical plane or as complementary to their spouses and, thus, different from themselves, had little to do with satisfaction. Differences in personality and character traits which fuel complementarity may lead to conflicts of power and control in some marriages. If tempered by other factors in relationships such as respect and understanding, differences may have nurtured a sense of connection, mutuality, and equity with the spouse which were significant sources of satisfaction in the empty-nest years.

Satisfaction was not related to age of respondents, a finding that differed from the findings of Levenson et al. (1993). We used approximately the same age groupings as in their study (forties, fifties, sixties, and seventies), although our modes of data collection, definition of variables, and diversity of respondents were different. We also found no relationship between years married (under 30, 30–40, and over 40 years) and marital satisfaction.

Consistent with the findings of Levenson et al. (1993), there was no significant relationship between the number of children and satisfaction in the post-parenting years. In addition, although marital conflict had become more severe in the child-rearing years, only minimal conflict was associated with parenting in the empty-nest years.

There were no differences between the sexes in the level of satisfaction, although men spoke somewhat differently than women about their thoughts and feelings. When wives talked about satisfaction, many spoke of the whole relationship by mentioning both positive and negative aspects. Men, on the other hand, talked mostly in positive terms about satisfaction, especially when they expressed what their spouses meant to them. That is, several husbands were satisfied without reservations, while wives were satisfied within the context of relationships that were experienced as having mostly good and satisfying elements along with imperfections. These subtle variations on the theme of satisfaction were similar to the findings of Fowers (1991).

Social and cultural variables played a marginal role in shaping marital satisfaction. However, educational level, income, religion, and ethnicity did have a more influential effect on satisfaction than age, years married, number of children, and gender. Blue-collar respondents reported higher levels of satisfaction in the post-parenting phase than did white-collar college graduates [$p = .09$]. Ninety percent of noncollege graduates were satisfied with their marriages compared to 79 percent of respondents who had graduated from college. Those with the highest family incomes (over

$100,000) and those with the lowest family incomes (under $25,000) were the most satisfied [*p* = .02]. Respondents in the middle-income range ($50,000 to $75,000) expressed the most dissatisfaction; 30 percent of that income group were negative or clearly ambivalent about their marriages. Ninety-four percent of Catholics were satisfied with their marriages, compared to 83 percent of Jews and 78 percent of Protestants [*p* = .07]. That pattern may have been shaped by ethnicity since 100 percent of Mexican Americans, all of whom were Catholic, were satisfied with their marriages, followed by 86 percent of African Americans and 81 percent of whites [*p* = .07].

Although the factors discussed so far had an influential effect on marital satisfaction in the empty-nest years, the more powerful forces contributing to satisfaction were in the relationships themselves. Five clusters of factors (conflict, decision making, communication, relational values, and intimacy) were found to be essential components of satisfaction in these marriages.

CONFLICT

The level of interpersonal conflict had a significant effect on satisfaction throughout the three phases of marriage. The most conflictual period was during the child-rearing years when major conflict was reported by 29 percent of respondents compared to 13 percent in the beginning phase. By the third phase of marriage, major conflict was reported by 7 percent of respondents. During that phase, 99 percent of respondents who were satisfied with their marriages reported minimal conflict [$X^2 (1, N = 120) = 37.91$, $p = .001$].

Two dynamics were critical in understanding the relationship between conflict and satisfaction. One dynamic was related to the seriousness of conflict. Major difficulties, defined as conflicts that had a highly disruptive effect on marital relationships, were clearly associated with lower satisfaction. When they remained unresolved, major conflicts had an eroding effect on the quality of relationships. As others have found (Argyle & Furnhan, 1983; Gottman & Krokoff, 1989; Vaillant & Vaillant, 1993), unresolved conflict reinforced negative interactions between spouses, which bred dissatisfaction. The resulting defensive behaviors perpetuated further conflict and estrangement between spouses. When that cycle was not interrupted and continued into the post-parenting years, spouses felt unhappy about their relationships.

The shift toward more adaptive and less defensive modes of dealing with major conflicts, especially those that erupted during the child-rearing years, contributed to marital satisfaction in the empty-nest phase. During the latter phase, major conflict declined significantly from the previous phase. In part, that change was attributed to the reality of children reaching adulthood, since many major conflicts were related to differences in parenting. The catalyst for major conflict was no longer present; couples also had distance from the source of conflict, which aided in the transition to a new phase in their marriages.

Another source of post-parenting satisfaction in the marriages was found in the modes used by many spouses to resolve differences. Confrontation or face-to-face discussion became the vehicle for resolving conflicts in the empty-nest years, a shift that began during the latter years of parenting. Confrontation had a containing effect on the severity of conflict, but only if it was grounded in other attributes of relationships such as mutual trust, respect, and understanding. Continued avoidance may have inflamed feelings of unhappiness and prolonged serious conflict. What we call empathic confrontations appeared to have beneficial effects on the long-term quality of relationships that have been reported by others (Gottman & Krokoff, 1989; Haefner, Notarias, & Pelligrini, 1991). Positive results interrupted the potential downward spiral in negative interactions and estrangements. Self-esteem was enhanced as well as feelings of connection with the spouses. The process had a containing effect on marital conflicts; that is, confrontation kept conflicts at a manageable level and neutralized the eroding effect of chronic unhappiness on satisfaction. Confronting differences and talking about conflicts enhanced feelings of mutuality as relationships matured.

DECISION MAKING

Mutuality in decision making increased significantly from the early years of marriage through the empty-nest years, involving specifically decisions about friends, leisure activities, and major purchases. Satisfaction rose proportionately with the shift toward mutuality in decision making. Early in marriage, 63 percent of respondents said that they and their spouses made decisions jointly, a figure that rose to 82 percent during the empty-nest years. By the third phase of marriage, respondents who talked of making decisions together rather than separately were more satisfied with their marriages [X^2 (1, $N = 120$) = 10.92, $p = .001$].

The parenting years were instrumental in the steady increase toward mutuality of decision making. As husbands became more involved in parenting, especially as children became adolescents, joint decisions about setting limits and discipline became increasingly common. Making decisions about children brought many spouses together. The mutuality that characterized child-rearing carried over to other decisions as well. Parenting became another vehicle on the road to mutuality in marital relationships which was an important nutriment in satisfaction.

COMMUNICATION

Reports about the quality of communication from the beginning of marriage through the parenting years were mixed. Forty-three percent of respondents in phase one and 46 percent in phase two described the communicative aspect of their relationships in positive terms such as open, comfortable, and direct. About the same number of respondents said that their communication was "O.K." but "could have been a lot better"; that is, having an open and honest discussion with the spouse about the marital relationship was mixed, with good and not so good memories. Only 15 percent of respondents remembered "little or no" communication in the early years, which declined to 7 percent during child-rearing.

Respondents were satisfied with their marriages even when memories about communication were mixed. However, poor communication contributed significantly to dissatisfaction. Of those respondents who were satisfied with their marriages in the post-parenting years, 80 percent described communication in positive terms. Among the 14 percent of respondents who were dissatisfied during that phase, none described communication in positive terms [X^2 (1, $N = 120$) = 42.74, $p = < .001$].

Change toward positive communication in the post-parenting years was part of an overall pattern of change toward expressiveness which contributed to satisfaction. The more respondents talked to their spouses of how they felt about a wide range of issues, the higher the satisfaction with their marriage. By the third phase, 63 percent of the role behaviors of respondents within marital relationships were described in expressive terms compared to 49 percent at the beginning of marriage. Husbands changed more than wives who were described as both expressive and instrumental throughout marriage. Those who made the shift toward integrating expressive behavior as part of their marital roles were more satisfied than those who maintained mainly instrumental modes of relating to the spouse.

Shifts toward expressiveness were on a modest scale; they did not involve grand changes in the way one behaved generally in relationships. Nor did they suggest major modifications in personality. In becoming expressive, one found words to share feelings about aspects of the marital relationship or other matters important to both spouses. Shifts of this kind were incremental as well as selective.

Relating predominantly through instrumental means without expressing feelings did not change for 14 percent of respondents throughout marriage. Their mixed to dissatisfied reactions to marriage remained constant throughout the three phases. The constancy of this theme throughout marriage suggests a character trait that was stable and predictive of satisfaction (Kelly & Conley, 1987).

Communication was an inherent part of relationships. Spouses communicated about conflicts, decisions, sex, and many other issues. It was important to explore the quality of marital communication in relation to these specific aspects of marriage. In some areas, communication was perceived as "good," but "not so good" in others. Respondents offered assessments as well on the overall quality of communication in their marriages. Mark and Melinda, who had been married for thirty-two years, spoke of the quality of communication in their marriage. Implicit in their observation was the relationship of communication to satisfaction. Mark observed that

> We generally feel comfortable in sharing. For myself, however, I recognize some of the things that bother her. It may be a question of timing when I may say something. If it's something that I might think will be stressful to her, I might not bring it up now. I may bring it up at a later point ... but if there's something that's real different, we talk about it ... if it's something I think she feels strongly about, I say: "OK, that's the way it's going to be. What you say is OK." And vice versa ... the talking might not be as direct on some issues right away. I think we still try to communicate ... still with the reservation that I have in terms of what I can share ... one of the key things is how much we talk about things and share ... more and more you learn what each other likes.

A similar assessment was offered by his wife, Melinda, who also said that communication had improved in their later years. She acknowledged that the quality of communication had changed for the better, which had enhanced satisfaction with the marriage:

> I think that communication also is very good, but it hasn't always been that good. There were times when it was not bad communication, it was just not much communication, particularly about things that were important and needed to be talked about. We just sort of went along and it just went along

too, and of course sat there. But I think that we've developed to the point now where there's very good communication.

RELATIONAL VALUES

Relational values refer to qualities that respondents were asked to assess in themselves and their spouses. These qualities were trust, respect, empathic understanding, and equity. Satisfaction was correlated significantly with these relational values, which have been viewed as critical to marital stability and satisfaction (Allen & Thompson, 1984; Kelley & Burgoon, 1991; Lauer, Lauer, & Kerr, 1990).

Two themes were evident in the perceptions of trust, respect, and empathic understanding. One was that satisfaction was associated more positively with how respondents assessed these qualities in their spouses than in themselves. In other words, one's satisfaction was shaped more by how the spouses trusted, respected, and understood the respondent than the other way around. That dissimilarity was characteristic of the earlier phases of marriage and disappeared by the empty-nest years. In that phase, mutual trust, respect and empathic understanding contributed significantly to marital satisfaction [$p = < .001$].

A second theme was related to what appeared to be growth in these qualities throughout marriage. Mutual respect was constant, while trust and understanding developed over the three phases of marriage. Respect for the spouse as well as an assessment of the spouse's respect for her or him appeared to be an antecedent quality (Kelly & Conley, 1987) which may have been strengthened, but did not change substantively, throughout marriage. Trust appeared to be a quality that needed to be worked out during the early marital years. Mutual trust was not significantly associated with satisfaction until the parenting years. Empathic understanding developed as relationships evolved and did not contribute significantly to satisfaction until the post-parenting years. During that phase, all three of these qualities became mutually influential in shaping satisfaction.

Several researchers have identified equity or a sense of fairness as important to marital happiness and satisfaction (Aida & Falbo, 1991; Broderick & O'Leary, 1986; Kelly & Burgoon, 1991). Despite the conflicts and differences that couples experienced through the child-rearing years, over 60 percent reported that "things balanced out" in their relationships. By the empty-nest years, 81 percent of respondents reported that their relationships were fair to them. Equity was a significant factor in nurturing satisfaction. A sense of fairness contributed to satisfaction even during the child-rearing years when wives experienced relationships as least equitable of the three phases. By the empty-nest years, nine out of ten respondents who were satisfied with their marriages assessed them as equitable; of those respondents who were not satisfied, four out of ten assessed them as equitable [X^2 (1, $N = 120$) $=20.10$, $p = < .001$].

A sense of fairness usually did not emerge unless spouses accepted responsibility for identifying, discussing, and mediating differences and inequities. The following couple described that process. Kiko was responding to a question about his perceptions of fairness in the marriage. He thought that the relationship was fair for him but not for his wife, Krystal:

> For me it has been fair, but I don't think it has for her. I would like for her to feel fully happy but I don't think she is. I can't find a way to convince her that I make everything to stay together and this is her big concern ... it's not fair to her because of my work I think it balanced out ... whenever one of us starts to feel that it's unbalanced, then we say so and work out something.

Krystal described the change in her sense of fairness about their marriage:

> I think it's fair now. . . . I gave him all the power in the beginning. It's like the first ten or twelve years I was behind him. . . . I was letting him go and I was taking care of my kids, but little by little I was turning things around; now we're this way. . . if I had been this way in the beginning . . .

Krystal did not complete her thought, but we may infer, from other parts of the interview, that the marriage was now more satisfying than it had been in previous years and that was related to changes which resulted in a more equitable relationship.

INTIMACY

Intimacy included both physical and psychological dimensions. We have already discussed how intimacy changed throughout the three phases of marriage. As people grew older, the frequency of sexual relations declined and the quality of psychological intimacy improved.

By the post-parenting years, sex continued to play an important role in shaping marital satisfaction. Of those respondents who were satisfied with their marriages (86 percent of the sample), 63 percent described sexual relations in positive terms and 37 percent used negative or ambivalent language in describing sexual relations. With one exception, respondents who were not satisfied with marriage were not satisfied with sex [X^2 (1, N

= 120) = 19.31, $p = < .001$]. Correspondingly, if sex was important to respondents, it was also important to marital satisfaction [X^2 (1, $N = 120$) = 20.23, $p = < .001$].

Physical touching or being demonstrative without sexual intercourse remained relatively constant throughout the three phases. Approximately half of the sample reported regular touching. Spouses who touched regularly were more satisfied with marriage than those who engaged in little or no touching. By the third phase, 60 percent of respondents who were satisfied with marriage reported regular touching; those who were not satisfied with their relationships reported little or no touching [X^2 (1, $N = 120$) = 21.17, $p = < .001$].

Psychological intimacy changed considerably during the post-parenting years. Up to that phase, sharing private, inner parts of oneself with a spouse was reported by about half of respondents. By the empty-nest phase, 73 percent experienced their relationships as psychologically intimate. Eighty-five percent of respondents who were satisfied with their marriages during those years described their relationships in psychologically intimate terms. None of the dissatisfied respondents described their relationships as psychologically intimate [X^2 (1, $N = 120$) = 54.47, $p = < .001$]. Of the three dimensions of intimacy explored in this study, psychological intimacy was the most significant contributor to satisfaction during the empty-nest years.

The theme of intimacy was evident in the responses of the following couple as they spoke of changes in that dimension of their thirty-five-year marriage. Implicit in what John said was the relationship between the development of psychological closeness and satisfaction with their relationship in the post-parenting years. Like many respondents, John used the word "friend" to convey what the relationship meant to him:

> I think we are good friends as well as partners ... like friends you do a lot more things together. You know what each other likes to do. The togetherness has gotten stronger. I feel closer to her. ... A lot of things still go unsaid but we know it's there.

Judy, his wife, spoke more specifically of the elements in their marriage which contributed to the changing sense of intimacy and resulting satisfaction:

> I think he's made me a better person because he's more understanding than I am. I just feel like I've grown from knowing him ... our marriage has changed from being a big romantic whirlwind thing to kind of long hard years with the kids, to a very nice time now. We're wise enough to appreciate just a

sunny day … You go into a marriage with crazy expectations, and I think you change with your children; there's so many pleasures that you didn't expect would come from having children, and we have so many satisfactions … and now we're appreciating each other more than ever … as I told you John used to be very quiet and keep things to himself for the first years of our marriage, and now he speaks right up. And if he doesn't like something he'll let me know … he would never do that before, he really wouldn't.

Judy identified qualities in her husband which enhanced her self-esteem despite his difficulties with expressing feelings. Child-rearing for these parents of five children was an important phase in the development of their relationship as a couple and set the stage for a different sense of intimacy during the post-parenting years. As with several husbands, John's shift toward expressiveness helped to sustain that new sense of intimacy.

CONCLUSIONS

These stable marriages had endured for a number of reasons, not the least of which was that the spouses were satisfied with their relationships. Differences between spouses had little impact on satisfaction, although equity or a sense of fairness in relationships despite differences had a significant effect on how satisfied respondents were with their relationships. Age, gender, number of years married, and number of children also had no significant impact on marital satisfaction. Educational level, our indicator of social class status, did have a marginal influence on satisfaction; blue-collar marriages as determined by the husbands' educational level were more satisfying in the empty-nest years than were white-collar marriages. Ethnicity, religion, and gross family income also had marginal effects in shaping satisfaction during the post-parenting years. Mexican Americans, all of whom were Catholic, reported the highest levels of satisfaction. With regard to income, couples with the lowest incomes, 71 percent of whom were Mexican Americans, and those with the highest incomes, 60 percent of whom were Jews, were the most satisfied during the third phase of marriage. Blue- and white-collar marriages in the mid-income ranges had the highest proportions of dissatisfaction.

There were five clusters of factors which had a significant effect on satisfaction: containment of conflict; mutuality in decision making; quality of communication; relational values of trust, respect, empathic under-standing and equity; and sexual and psychological intimacy. Marital conflict, which was contained to a relatively minor level in the third phase, was related significantly to satisfaction. This was an important finding since a substantial number of marriages had been affected adversely by major conflicts during the parenting years. An increase in face-to-face modes of dealing with conflict was a significant dynamic in that change. The trend toward mutuality in decision making as marriages matured contributed to satisfaction, as did openness and comfort with marital communication. Underlying these changes which nurtured satisfaction were values on which relationships were grounded. These values, which became increasingly mutual as spouses lived out their lives together in middle and old age, included trust, respect, empathic communication, and a prevailing sense of fairness about relationships. All of these changes enhanced feelings of intimacy with one's spouse. Psychological intimacy or a sense of closeness with the spouse increased significantly in the post-parenting years in contrast to sexual intimacy, which declined for almost half of respondents.

As important as these factors were in understanding satisfaction as well as the stability of these marriages, there were other aspects which came up repeatedly in our interviews. Although they have been implicit in our discussion thus far, these factors merit explicit attention before we close this exploration of these long-lasting marriages. They are adaptability, resiliency, and commitment.

More than anything else, this book has been about change and about how people adapted to change in the most important relationships of their lives. One of the remarkable aspects of this research for two professionals, who have spent major portions of their careers doing marital therapy or preparing others to treat marital conflict, was in gaining a deeper appreciation of how people helped themselves. The subjects in this study changed throughout their marriages without professional intervention. As we listened to people talk about changes that had happened within them and in their marital relationships, we developed a renewed respect for how people adapt to, rather than defend against, change. More than ever, we are reminded that clients really help themselves, and the therapist is but a catalyst in the process of change. Many people have indigenous resources that they use constructively in the interest of adaptation. Family, churches, and friends are invaluable resources for helping couples build a satisfying marriage.

One component of adaptation is related to the way in which individuals frame their perceptions of reality. Respondents may have emphasized the positive aspects of their relationships and deemphasized the negative ones. In referring to cognitive consistency theory, Spanier et al. (1975) speculated that couples in long-lasting relationships may put a positive spin on their thoughts and feelings. Framing reality in that way offers one a rationale for staying in a relationship. We have no way of knowing how much the need to be cognitively consistent shaped the observations of respondents. The quality of the data suggested that this was not a significant dynamic in shaping the reports of respondents. The stories that we were privileged to hear contained a range of observations about the quality of marital relationships. Although some respondents may have put a positive spin on their thoughts and feelings, their observations of themselves and their spouses suggested a balanced and candid perception of reality.

Resiliency, or the capacity of people to recover from adversity, was another hidden dynamic that contributed to marital satisfaction. Many people in this study suffered from the stresses associated with poverty, racism, life threatening illnesses, physical impairments, and emotional conflicts. Marital relationships were a resource for helping individuals cope with these adversities. Implicit in these findings was the critical role that loving relationships played in helping individuals to face painful realities and to overcome their painful effects on the human spirit. The most frequently used word to capture the special quality or meaning of the spouse was that of "friend." Supportive relationships, especially happy and satisfying marriages, contribute enormously to supporting the natural resiliency within individuals. Genuine support within a loving relationship characterized by trust, respect, and understanding often enabled couples to negotiate through the most difficult of times. Being able to survive losses and other threats to individual well-being with a special friend was a great source of satisfaction.

Respondents used the word "commitment" as much as friendship as they talked about stability and satisfaction. As adaptable and resilient as these people were in their marriages, it was the assuring sense of being together, no matter what happened over the years, that often held relationships together. They were of an era when wedding vows meant that marriages were not severed as readily as they are today. Many respondents talked as if they had no alternatives such as divorce. Fidelity to the marriage was their only option. Quite apart from the containing effect of commitment on marital stability was the meaning of commitment to a relationship of mutual love. If one truly loved another, this was sufficient reason to spend a lifetime together. In one way or another, this thought was an inherent part of being married.

We close this book with passages from the interviews of a couple who were married for thirty-seven years. As they spoke of the depth of their evolving love for one another, themes of adaptability, resiliency, and commitment emerged. Douglas remembered times of major conflict when

The communication was broken down; it started breaking down real bad. She started going her own way and I started going mine, and it went that way for quite a while ... it almost tore us apart. We were just living and staying under the same roof ... today, every day ain't peaches and cream, but it's a lot better than what it used to be. We laugh and talk about some of the things that almost broke our marriage up, all kinds of stuff. And I know she loves me and she knows that I love her. We just know that about each other ... in my own way of thinking, I loved her all along but I didn't know how to say it ... now I can say it but I still get a funny feeling. And I know it's true you know. It's just that I never knew what love was. When she hurts or has pain or something, it bothers me. I don't think I even cared; I didn't know how to. So, I almost drove her completely away from me ... I think about it even now, but I don't let it bother me because there's nothing I can do about it ... we talk about some of that stuff now, and laugh about it. I think it really brought us closer together.... Sometimes I'll be laying in bed at night and I'll just be running this through my mind. And I think that God must have wanted us to be together. With all the turmoil ... we're still together today, and we love one another and care about one another more now than we did when we first started ... the closeness has improved greatly over the last two or three years; we're more understanding and more respectful of one another. We've become like one. She means my whole life to me right now ... when one of us has to go, pass away, I hope that it would be me. I want to go first ... that's how much I love her ...

Remembering her expectations of marriage as a young bride, Della commented that

most people who do go into marriage feel like the storybook romance is going to go on forever. But it doesn't. It's a thin line between love and hate. You can love in a marriage and you can hate in a marriage. But you got to be able to recognize it: "It's OK for me to hate. It's OK for me to love. It's OK if I tell you to go to hell. Fine, maybe tomorrow I won't." I had to learn that myself as I grew with him. I said these vows to this man, and half of them, I didn't mean because that was my ticket for out of the house. My love grew. ... that's great in a marriage if two people can say: "It's OK, we can grow with one another" ... We've had good times and we've had bad times. But that's life, you know ... I think the best thing in life about two people is when they're able to come back and say, "I'm sorry," or "I did see it wrong." He has been a real human being for me ... as we grew, we grew stronger. I knew that he was good ... you can feel when people love you. I just loved my husband and he loved me. There's been times in our lives when I could say: "I don't think this is what I want out of life." But we always sit down and we talk about it and we give it another go ... as you grow, and you're with someone for so long, you learn to get all that nurturing from them. He's my world. That's what he means to me. You know, the world out there is the world, but he's my world.

REFERENCES

Aida, Y., & Falbo, T. (1991). Relationships between marital satisfaction, resources, and power strategies. *Sex Roles, 24* (1/2), 43–56.

Allen, A., & Thompson, T. (1984). Agreement, understanding, realization, and feeling understood as predictors of communicative satisfaction in marital dyads. *Journal of Marriage and the Family* (November), 915–921.

Argyle, M., & Furnham, A. (1983). Sources of satisfaction and conflict in long-term relationships. *Journal of Marriage and the Family* (August), 481–493.

Broderick, J., & O'Leary, K. D. (1986). Contributions of affect, attitudes, and behavior to marital satisfaction. *Journal of Consulting and Clinical Psychology, 54* (4), 514–517.

Fowers, B. (1991). His and her marriages: A multivariate study of gender and marital satisfaction. *Sex Roles, 24* (3/4), 209–221.

Gottman, J., & Krokoff, L. (1989). Marital interaction and satisfaction: A longitudinal view. *Journal of Consulting and Clinical Psychology, 57* (1), 47–52.

Haefner, P., Notarius, C., & Pellegrini, D. (1991). Determinants of satisfaction with marital discussions: An exploration of husband-wife differences. *Behavioral Assessment, 13*, 67–82.

Hicks, M. W., & Platt, M. (1970). Marital happiness and stability: A review of the research in the sixties. *Journal of Marriage and the Family, 32*, 553–574.

Kelley, D., & Burgoon, J. (1991). Understanding marital satisfaction and couple type as functions of relational expectations. *Human Communication Research, 18* (1), 40–69.

Kelly, E. L., & Conley, J. (1987). Personality and compatibility: A prospective analysis of marital stability and marital satisfaction. *Journal of Personality and Social Psychology, 52* (1), 27–40.

Lauer, R. H., & Lauer, J., & Kerr, S. T. (1990). The long-term marriage: Perceptions of stability and satisfaction. *International Journal of Aging and Human Development, 31* (3), 189–195.

Levenson, R., Carstensen, L., & Gottman, J. (1993). Long-term marriage: Age, gender and satisfaction. *Psychology and Aging, 8* (3), 301–313.

Lewis, R. A. & Spanier, G. B. (1979). Theorizing about the quality and stability of marriage. In W. R. Burr, R. Hill, F. I. New, & I. L. Reiss (Eds.), *Contemporary theories about the family* (pp. 268–294). Glencoe, IL: The Free Press.

Shachar, R. (1991). His and her marital satisfaction: The double standard. *Sex Roles, 25* (7/8), 451–467.

Spanier, G. B., & Lewis, R. A. (1980). Marital quality: A review of the seventies. *Journal of Marriage and the Family,* 825–839.

Spanier, G. B., Lewis, R. A., & Cole, C. L. (1975). Marital adjustment over the family life cycle: The issue of curvilinearity. *Journal of Marriage and the Family, 37,* (May), 263–275.

Vaillant, C., & Vaillant, G. (1993). Is the U-curve of marital satisfaction an illusion? A 40 year study of marriage. *Journal of Marriage and the Family, 55* (February), 230–239.

Appendixes

Appendix A
Characteristics of Respondents

PSEUDO NAME	#	AGE	SEX	EDUCATION	RELIGION	ETHNICITY	OCCUPATION	CHILDREN	YEARS MARRIED	INCOME
Andrew	1	7	M	H	C	W	T	3	3	3
Ann	2	7	F	H	C	W	H	3	3	3
Ben	3	5	M	C	C	W	O	1	3	4
Barbara	4	5	F	H	C	W	T	1	3	4
Carl	5	5	M	<C	P	A	T	3	3	3
Carol	6	5	F	<C	P	A	T	3	3	3
David	7	5	M	H	C	W	T	5	3	3
Donna	8	5	F	H	C	W	T	5	3	3
Edward	9	4	M	H	P	W	U	3	2	2
Eve	10	4	F	H	C	W	T	3	3	2
Fred	11	6	M	H	C	W	U	5	3	2
Fran	12	6	F	<H	P	W	B	5	4	2
George	13	6	M	H	P	A	B	3	4	2
Grace	14	6	F	H	P	A	T	3	2	2
Ivan	15	4	M	H	C	W	P	3	2	3
Irene	16	4	F	C	C	W	T	3	3	3
John	17	5	M	H	C	W	P	5	3	3
Judy	18	5	F	<C	C	W	U	5	2	3
Ken	19	5	M	H	C	W	T	3	2	3
Karen	20	5	F	H	C	W	T	3	3	3
Larry	21	5	M	H	C	W	T	3	3	3
Laura	22	5	F	H	C	W	P	3	4	2
Mike	23	7	M	C	C	W	H	3	4	2
Mary	24	6	F	H	P	W	B	1	2	3
Al	25	4	M	<C	P	W	O	1	2	3
Arlene	26	4	F	C	P	W	B	1	2	5
Bill	27	4	M	C	P	W	B	1	2	5
Brenda	28	4	F	C	P	W	P	3	2	4
Calvin	29	5	M	C	O	W	B	3	2	4
Cathy	30	5	F	C	P	W	P	5	4	2
Donald	31	6	M	C	P	W	H	5	4	2
Doreen	32	6	F	<C	P	W	B	1	2	3
Earl	33	5	M	C	P	W	B	1	2	3
Evelyn	34	5	F	C	P	W	B	1	2	3

APPENDIX A

PSEUDO NAME	#	AGE	SEX	EDUCATION	RELIGION	ETHNICITY	OCCUPATION	CHILDREN	YEARS MARRIED	INCOME
Frank	35	7	M	C	P	W	B	1	4	2
Faith	36	7	F	C	P	W	P	1	4	2
Grover	37	5	M	C	J	W	P	3	3	5
Gladys	38	5	F	H	J	W	O	3	3	5
Kevin	39	5	M	C	J	W	B	1	2	5
Kate	40	5	F	C	P	W	B	1	2	5
Ian	41	6	M	C	J	W	B	5	4	3
Irene	42	6	F	<C	P	W	B	5	4	3
Jeff	43	6	M	C	J	W	P	3	3	4
Jill	44	5	F	C	J	W	P	3	2	4
Howard	45	5	M	C	P	W	P	1	2	4
Holly	46	5	F	C	P	W	P	1	3	4
Louis	47	6	M	C	C	W	B	3	3	5
Lilly	48	5	F	<C	C	W	B	3	5	1
Jorge	51	7	M	<H	C	M	U	3	5	1
Josephina	52	7	F	<H	C	M	U	3	3	2
Beto	53	5	M	<H	C	M	O	3	3	2
Buena	54	5	F	<C	C	M	O	3	4	1
Carlos	55	6	M	<H	C	M	U	1	4	1
Cenci	56	6	F	H	C	M	U	5	2	1
Dimos	57	7	M	<H	C	M	U	5	2	1
Dora	58	5	F	H	C	M	U	3	3	2
Esteban	59	5	M	H	C	M	T	3	3	2
Esperanza	60	5	F	H	C	M	O	1	2	3
Francisco	61	4	M	<C	C	M	T	1	2	3
Felicidad	62	4	F	C	C	M	P	3	2	3
Gonzalo	63	4	M	<H	C	M	U	3	2	1
Guadalupe	64	4	F	<C	C	M	O	3	2	2
Homero	65	4	M	H	C	M	B	1	2	2
Herminia	66	4	F	<C	C	M	P	1	2	2
Kiko	67	4	M	H	C	M	O	3	2	2
Krystal	68	4	F	<C	C	M	U	3	2	2
Ignacio	69	5	M	<H	C	M	U	5	2	2
Isabel	70	5	F	<H	C	M	U	5	2	2

APPENDIX A

PSEUDO NAME	#	AGE	SEX	EDUCATION	RELIGION	ETHNICITY	OCCUPATION	CHILDREN	YEARS MARRIED	INCOME
Armondo	71	6	M	H	C	M	U	5	3	1
Alicia	72	5	F	H	C	M	H	5	3	1
Martin	73	5	M	H	C	M	B	5	3	2
Maribel	74	5	F	C	C	M	B	5	3	2
Arthur	75	5	M	C	J	W	R	3	3	5
Allison	76	5	F	C	J	W	H	3	3	5
Brian	77	6	M	C	J	W	P	1	4	4
Bernice	78	6	F	C	J	W	D	1	4	4
Clifton	79	7	M	C	J	W	B	3	4	5
Cora	80	6	F	C	J	W	P	3	4	5
Daniel	81	6	M	C	J	W	B	3	4	3
Debra	82	6	F	C	J	W	H	3	4	3
Earl	83	7	M	C	J	W	B	1	5	5
Emily	84	7	F	C	J	W	H	1	5	5
Freeman	85	7	M	C	J	W	B	1	4	5
Fannie	86	6	F	H	J	W	H	1	4	5
Greg	87	6	M	C	J	W	B	3	4	5
Gail	88	6	F	H	J	W	H	3	4	5
Henry	89	5	M	C	J	W	B	1	2	5
Hillary	90	4	F	H	J	W	B	1	2	5
Len	91	6	M	C	J	W	P	3	4	4
Lillian	92	6	F	H	J	W	H	3	4	4
Joseah	93	5	M	C	J	W	P	1	3	5
Julia	94	5	F	H	J	W	B	1	3	5
Isaac	95	5	M	C	J	W	B	1	2	4
Ina	96	5	F	C	J	W	P	1	2	4
Kent	97	4	M	C	J	W	B	1	2	4
Kim	98	4	F	C	J	W	B	1	2	4
Art	101	6	M	C	C	A	P	5	4	3
Amy	102	6	F	C	C	A	P	5	4	3
Bob	103	7	M	H	C	A	B	3	5	2
Beth	104	6	F	H	P	A	B	3	5	2
Corey	105	7	M	H	P	A	U	3	4	1
Carmela	106	6	F	H	P	A	U	3	4	1

APPENDIX A

PSEUDO NAME	#	AGE	SEX	EDUCATION	RELIGION	ETHNICITY	OCCUPATION	CHILDREN	YEARS MARRIED	INCOME
Douglas	107	6	M	<H	C	A	U	3	3	2
Della	108	5	F	H	C	A	O	3	3	2
Eugene	109	7	M	H	C	A	U	1	2	1
Edith	110	7	F	<H	C	A	U	1	2	1
Felix	111	7	M	<H	P	A	U	3	5	2
Fay	112	7	F	<H	P	A	H	3	5	2
Guy	113	7	M	<H	P	A	U	1	3	2
Gloria	114	7	F	H	P	A	U	1	3	2
Harold	115	5	M	H	P	A	U	5	3	2
Heidi	116	5	F	H	P	A	B	5	3	2
Irwin	117	7	M	H	P	A	O	3	4	2
Iris	118	7	F	H	P	A	H	3	4	2
Justin	119	5	M	H	P	A	B	3	3	3
Jane	120	5	F	H	P	A	B	3	3	3
Kirk	121	7	M	<H	P	A	T	1	5	2
Kirsten	122	7	F	<H	P	A	H	1	5	2
Mark	125	6	M	C	P	A	H	1	3	3
Melinda	126	6	F	C	P	A	P	1	3	3

LEGEND   Please note: Names have been changed in order to protect the privacy of respondents

AGE
4 = 40-49
5 = 50-59
6 = 60-69
7 = 70-79

EDUCATION
<H = Less than High School
HS = High School Graduate
<C = Some College or Post High School
C = College Graduate

OCCUPATION
B = Business   P = Professional
H = At Home   T = Trade
O = Other   U = Unskilled Work

RELIGION
C = Catholic
J = Jewish
P = Protestant

CHILDREN
1 = 1 or 2
3 = 3 or 4
5 = 5 or more

ETHNICITY
A = African-American
M = Mexican-American
W = White

YEARS MARRIED
2 = 20 - 29 years
3 = 30 - 39 years
4 = 40 or more

INCOME
1 = UNDER 25, 000
2 = 25,000 - 49,999
3 = 50,000 - 74,999
4 = 75,000 - 99,999
5 = >100,000

Appendix B
Methodology

This study explored how husbands and wives adapted to each other from early years of marriage, through the parenting years, and into the post-parenting or empty-nest years. The investigation used a qualitative and phenomenological research approach in studying the marital histories of 120 spouses (i.e., respondents) from sixty marriages. Based on grounded theory methodology (Strauss & Corbin, 1990), data were elicited from the perspective of individual spouses in order to develop an understanding of how they adapted to marriage over the life of their relationships. Semistructured interviews with each spouse focused on the changing nature of marital relationships from the initial stage of their relationships, through child-rearing, and into the mature years (see Appendix C for Interview Guide).

SAMPLE

The sample was purposively chosen to fit with the goal of developing an understanding of adaptation among couples in long-lasting relationships. Principles of theoretical sensitivity were adopted in choosing the sample (Strauss & Corbin, 1990). Because of underrepresentation in previous research on marriage, couples were recruited who met the following criteria:

1. Married at least twenty years

2. Youngest child at least 18 years and/or out of high school

3. No current psychotherapy or history of extensive marriage counseling

4. Racial, ethnic, educational, and religious diversity

For a summary of the characteristics of each respondent, see Appendix A.

The researchers recruited couples through business, professional, and trade union organizations; churches and synagogues; and a variety of other community organizations. Most couples resided in the Northeast with the exception of Mexican Americans who resided in the Southwest.

The 120 respondents were separated according to the three independent variables in the study:

A. Ethnicity/Race
White	68 (.57)
African American	28 (.23)
Mexican American	24 (.20)

B. Religious Background
Catholic	50 (.42)
Protestant	40 (.33)

Jewish	30 (.25)

C. Education
College Graduate	42 (.35)
Noncollege Graduate	78 (.65)

By age, 16 percent of respondents were in their forties; 20 percent in their seventies; and 54 percent in their fifties and sixties. Twenty-seven percent of couples had been married over forty-years; 42 percent between thirty and forty years; and 32 percent less than thirty years. Thirty-five percent of couples had one or two children; 47 percent had three or four; and 18 percent had five or more. By total family income, approximately 12 percent of couples earned less than $25,000 and 19 percent over $100,000. Thirty-two percent had family incomes between $25,000 and $49,999; 25 percent between $50,000 and $74,999; and 12 percent between $75,000 and $99,999.

FORMAT AND PROCEDURES

The interview format was developed after a review of the marriage literature (Barry, 1970; Gottman & Krokoff, 1989; Hicks & Platt, 1970; Kelly & Conley, 1987; Lewis & Spanier, 1979; Rubin, 1983; Spanier & Fleer, 1980). The semistructured interview was developed and pretested by the researchers. Collaborative researchers conducted additional pilot testing and provided feedback from couples, which led to further refinement of the interview guide. After this preliminary work, the guide was divided into four major sections: the relationship; social influences, including social, economic, and cultural factors; their parents' marriages; and respondents' experiences and views of their marriages over time. Each interview section was subdivided into three developmental stages: the initial years of marriage prior to children, the child-rearing years, and post–child-rearing or the empty-nest years. The goal of the semistructured interview was to acquire in-depth information about intergenerational, interpersonal, gender, ethnic, economic, and communication factors in long-term marriages. Spouses were asked about their roles, needs, expectations, sense of relatedness to each other, problem-solving abilities, and the overall equity as well as quality of their marriages as their relationships evolved. An open-ended style of interviewing was followed to allow for freedom of expression (Kvale, 1983).

Focal questions were used to elicit information from the unique perspectives of each respondent. Interviews allowed for flexibility and openness; they were exploratory and discovery-oriented (Moon, Dillon, & Sprenkle, 1990; Strauss & Corbin, 1990), which allowed the couples to express the meanings and the processes of their marital interactions within their own frame of reference. That approach, which adapted clinical interviewing skills to the needs of the research, allowed the researchers to explore the complexities of the marital adjustments and interactions as the couples remembered and reported them.

The interviewers were advanced doctoral students with extensive clinical experience. They were sensitive to and respectful of respondents and accepting of the uniqueness of each individual's perceptions of marital relationships. In that respect, professional, empathic interviewing skills were a valuable resource in collecting the data.

The interviews were held in the homes of the respondents, which provided additional information about their life-styles and environments. Prior to each interview, respondents were told about the purpose of the study, given an overview of the interview schedule, and were assured their identities would remain anonymous. Informed consent for audiotaping and the research use of interviews was obtained. Each spouse was interviewed separately; the length of each of the interviews was approximately two hours.

CODING

The interviews were transcribed to facilitate accurate coding and to prepare the data for both quantitative and qualitative analysis. A scoring system was developed to identify themes that evolved from each section of the interview. There were over ninety categories in twenty-four topic areas; rating scores were obtained for each of the three phases of the marriage (initial, child-rearing, and later years).

Each interview was coded independently by two raters (one male and one female) who noted categories and themes as they emerged from the transcripts of interviews. One of the authors coded all 120 interviews to ensure continuity in operational definitions of variables and consistency of judgments from interview to interview. The raters then met together to review their independent codes. Areas of disagreement, which occurred less than 13 percent of the time, were discussed and resolved by the two raters. Thus, there was an agreed upon scoring response for each category.

DATA ANALYSIS

The coded data were analyzed using the Statistical Package for the Social Sciences (SPSS, 1990). Interview variables were of a nominal level so that the use of nonparametric statistics (chi-square) enabled the research team to identify significant patterns and changes in marital relationships over time. Quantitative analysis offered direction to the qualitative analysis. The latter included the use of Hyperesearch software (1991), which the researchers used to identify, catalogue, and organize specific interview passages on which quantitative codes had been based. Hyperesearch was a highly efficient and reliable tool in the qualitative analysis of data. The software allowed us to do a thorough content analysis of the 120 transcriptions of tape-recorded interviews, which totaled over 4,000 double-spaced pages.

Appendix C
Interview Guide: African-American Couples

Introduction:

Thank you for being in the study. Brief explanation of the project. Read and sign consent form.

Explain structure of the interview:

1. Background information.
2. Your marriage as it was when you were first married and how it has stayed the same as well as how it has changed in terms of roles, expectations, and needs.
3. The issue of being African American, and the influence of cultural, religious, and socioeconomic factors on your marriage.
4. A look at your own family background and values and how these influenced your marriage.
5. The influence of your parent's marriage on your own marriage in terms of roles, expectations, and relating.
6. Your assessment of the important factors in your marriage over time.

Background Data:

Name: _____   Date of Birth: _____

Occupation: _____   Income: _____

Educational Level: _____

Children:

Names   Birth Dates

_____

_____

_____

_____

Other People Living in the Home:

Names   Relationship

_____

_____

Geog. Origins: _____   Religion: _____

Date of Marriage: _____

Spouse's Name and Birthdate: _____

I. **The Relationship**
    A. Initial attraction, life circumstances, family reactions.
        1. As you look back to the time when you met (spouse), what first attracted you to him/her? What do you think attracted him/her to you?
            a. What interests did you share?
            b. How long did you date before you decided to get married?
            c. Did any African American traditions influence your dating?
            d. How were you sure you wanted to marry (spouse)?
        2. How did your family feel about and react to (spouse)?
            a. Tell me about your family's reaction to your marriage (feelings of approval or disapproval).
            b. How did your family's reaction affect your decision to marry (spouse)?
        3. How did (spouse's) family react to the marriage?
            a. How much of an impact did their reaction have on your plans to get married?
        4. What was going on in your life around the time of your marriage educationally, vocationally, family, etc.?
            a. Who did you live with when first married?
        5. What kind of role did you see yourself playing in the relationship?
            a. What about (spouse's) role? (Expected, actual, changes).
            b. Did you expect to have to work at the relationship? Why?
    B. Roles, expectations, problem-solving, issues of relatedness and equity in the beginning, during child-rearing, and post-childrearing. (Ask the following questions in relation to the early years, the child-rearing and the empty-nest years.)
        1. Can you tell us how you and (spouse) got along?
            a. In general?
            b. What has been important to getting along? Sense of humor?
            c. How would you describe the communcation between you?

2. How did you go about making decisions and solving problems?
   (Re: work, friends, recreation, where to live, etc.)
   a. How did you handle differences (values, career, sex, etc.)?
   b. How would you describe your problem-solving style as compared to (spouse's)?
   c. Is there one particular area of conflict which stood out during each of the three phases of your marriage?
   d. Can you give me some examples of how you faced and dealt with crises (health, financial, etc.)?
3. How did you handle child-rearing responsibilities? (early, latency, adolescence)
4. How do you feel about your relationship?
   a. Looking back, what has been good, not so good and/or bad about the relationship?
   b. How much understanding do you feel (spouse) has had of you? (differentiation, separateness, etc.)
   c. How much understanding have you had of (spouse)?
   d. How sensitive has (spouse) been to you? And you to him/her?
   e. How much respect do you feel (spouse) has had for you? And you for him/her?
   f. How much trust have you felt for (spouse)?
   g. How much trust do you think (spouse) has felt towards you?
   h. How have you gotten along sexually? In terms of non-sexual intimacy like hugging and touching?
5. Overall, have you felt a sense of fairness in the marriage?
   a. Despite differences, have things balanced out?
   b. Do you feel that your ways of solving problems as a couple have been generally fair to each of you?
   c. Have there been situations where one of you had more influence than the other (money, friends, recreation, work, living, etc.)?

II. Socioeconomic Influences

How have the following played a role in your life together and how have they affected your marriage?

A. Religion
   1. How important has religion been in your life? What church activities do you participate in? How regularly?

2. How have your religious beliefs affected the way you cope with racism and discrimination?

B. Extended families.

    1. What influence has your family and your spouse's family had on your marriage?

C. Cultural factors including ethnicity and race.

    1. Do you feel that being a Black person in America has affected your marriage?

    2. How have you and (spouse) coped with discrimination and racism?

D. Economic factors, including income.

    1. Do you feel that you or (spouse) have ever been discriminated against in the workforce because of your race?

        a. How did you and (spouse) handle situation?

        b. Did it affect your relationship in any way?

    2. Do you feel that being a Black person has ever made it hard to provide financially for your family?

        a. If yes, how did this affected your relationship with (spouse)?

E. Are there other values, beliefs, or moral standards, that have played a role in your life together (Is there a motto that fits for you?)

    1. Are there any African American traditions or values that are part of your married/family life?

III. Parents' Marriage

A. What were your family's attitudes toward/experience with divorce?

B. What do you think you learned about marriage from observing your parents?

    1. How did you view your parents' relationship in terms of roles, relatedness, and equity?

    2. Can you tell me how your parents got along?

    3. How did they go about making decisions and solving problems? (Ask for some examples of how a disagreement was solved.)

        a. Despite differences did things balance out in their marriage?

        b. Did you feel that their ways of solving problems were generally fair to each partner? Were there situations where one of them had more influence than the other (money, friends, work, etc.)?

C. What are some important similarities in your marriage compared to your parents' marriage?

    1. What are some important differences?

2. Did your parents have any African American traditions that were a part of their marriage?

   a. If yes, do you follow these traditions in your own marriage?

IV. **Respondent's Views of the Marriage Over Time and WrapUp**

  A. As you look back, what were the personal qualities of (spouse) that kept you together?

    1. What other factors in the relationship kept you together?

    2. Were there any African American traditions that helped you to stay together?

  B. In what ways has your marriage changed over the years? How has it remained the same?

    1. How have your expectations changed or remained the same?

     a. How does what you are currently looking for in the relationship differ from your earlier expectations? (needs, roles, relatedness, communication)

  C. What words best describe what (spouse) means to you now? In the past?

  D. Are there any other things that you wish to add that were critical issues or factors that kept you in the relationship? Significant events, periods of assessment and/or renewal?

  E. Is there anything else that you think would be important for us to understand about your marriage, yourself, or your spouse?

    1. Anything else about your experience as an African American that would be important for us to know about?

Thank you!

Appendix D
Code Sheet: African-American Couples

interviewer:

interview date:

code # :

name:

income: ethnicity: occupation:

education: birth date: date of marriage:

spouse's name:

****

1.   Subject's initial attraction to spouse
     (0) negative (1) ambivalent (2) positive _____

2.   Subject's family support for spouse choice
     (1) disapproval (2) approval (3) mixed _____

3.   Subject's circumstances at time of marriage
     (0) no conflict (1) conflictual _____

4.   Role expectations of self in marriage
     (1) traditional (2) non-traditional _____

5.   S's expectation of need for effort to sustain marriage
     (0) no expectations (1) no (2) yes _____

6. Subject's perception of the sexual relationship

   (0) negative (1) mixed (2) positive

   (A) first phase   _____

   (B) second phase   _____

   (C) third phase   _____

7 S's perception of the importance of the sexual relationship

   (0) not important (1) important (2) very important

   (A) first phase   _____

   (B) second phase   _____

   (C) third phase   _____

8. S's perception of the presence of intimacy in the marriage (0) no (1) mixed (2) yes

   (A) psychosocial intimacy

   (1) first phase   _____

   (2) second phase   _____

   (3) third phase   _____

   (B) non-sexual physical touching

   (1) first phase   _____

   (2) second phase   _____

   (3) third phase   _____

9. S's personal style of decision making (0) logical (1) impulsive (2)intuitive

   (1) first phase   _____

   (2) second phase   _____

   (3) third phase   _____

10. External decision making style of the marriage couple (0) separate (1) variable (2) mutual
    (e. g. friends, recreation, vacations, purchases)

    (A) first phase   _____

    (B) second phase   _____

    (C) third phase   _____

11. Style of handling interpersonal diffrences in marriage (1) avoid (2) confront
    (A) Subject's style
    (1) first phase   _____
    (2) second phase   _____
    (3) third phase   _____
    (B) S's perception of spouse's style
    (1) first phase   _____
    (2) second phase   _____
    (3) third phase   _____

12. S's reported level of marital conflict (0) minimal (1) major
    (A) first phase   _____
    (B) second phase   _____
    (C) third phase   _____

13. S's perception of the responsibilities for child rearing (0) individual (1) mutual
    (A) children's infancy   _____
    (B) latency period   _____
    (C) adolescence   _____

14. S's perception of relationship variables: Spouse to Subject (0) no (1) mixed (2) yes
    (A) sensitivity
    (1) first phase _____ (2) second phase _____ (3) third phase _____
    (B) understanding

    (1) first phase _____ (2) second phase _____ (3) third phase _____
    (C) respect

    (1) first phase _____ (2) second phase _____ (3) third phase _____
    (D) trust

    (1) first phase _____ (2) second phase _____ (3) third phase _____

15. S's perception of relationship variables: Subject to Spouse (0) no (1) mixed (2) yes

(A) sensitivity

(1) first phase _____ (2) second phase _____ (3) third phase _____

(B) understanding

(1) first phase _____ (2) second phase _____ (3) third phase _____

(C) respect

(1) first phase _____ (2) second phase _____ (3) third phase _____

(D) trust

(1) first phase _____ (2) second phase _____ (3) third phase _____

16. S's perception of fairness/equity in the marital relationship (0) no (1) mixed (2) yes

(A) first phase   _____
(B) second phase   _____
(C) third phase   _____

17. S's perception of communication within the marital relationship (0) no (1) mixed (2) yes

(A) first phase   _____
(B) second phase   _____
(C) third phase   _____

18. Subject's overall sense of relatedness   (0) negative (1) mixed (2) positive

(A) first phase   _____
(B) second phase   _____
(C) third phase   _____

19. S's perception of other influences on the marriage

(0) negative (1) no influence (2) positive influence (3) mixed

(A) finances

(1) first phase _____ (2) second phase _____ (3) third phase _____

(B) religion

(1) first phase _____ (2) second phase _____ (3) third phase _____

(C) subject's extended family
(1) first phase _____ (2) second phase _____ (3) third phase _____
(D) spouse's extended family
(1) first phase _____ (2) second phase _____ (3) third phase _____
(E) culture/ethnicity
(1) first phase _____ (2) second phase _____ (3) third phase _____
(F) other values (list in comments)
(1) first phase _____ (2) second phase _____ (3) third phase _____

20. S's perception of similarity of own marriage with parents' marriage
     (0) discontinuity (1) mixed (2) continuity
     (A) first phase   _____
     (B) second phase   _____
     (C) third phase   _____

21. S's perception of own marital behavior   (0) instrumental (1) mixed (2) expressive
     (A) first phase   _____
     (B) second phase   _____
     (C) third phase   _____

22. S's parents' attitudes toward divorce
     (1) disapprove of divorce_____ (2) accepting of divorce _____

23. S's perception of interpersonal fit with spouse
     (1) mixed (2) complementarity (3) symmetry
     (A) first phase   _____
     (B) second phase   _____
     (C) third phase   _____

24. S's overall sense of the marriage as satisfying?   (0) no (1) mixed (2) yes
     (A) first phase   _____
     (B) second phase   _____
     (C) third phase   _____

25. S's perception of role of African American traditions in relationship   (1) no (2) yes
     (A) first phase   _____
     (B) second phase   _____
     (C) third phase   _____

26. Early living arrangement
     (1) with family _____
     (2) alone _____

27. Impact of early living arrangement
    (0)   no (1) negative (2) positive (3) mixed ____

28. S's perception of religion's role in coping with racism and discrimination
    (0) no (1) negative (2) positive ____

29. S's perceived style of coping with racism/discrimination
    (0)   mixed (1) avoid (2) confront
    (A)   first phase   _____
    (B)   second phase   _____
    (C)   third phase   _____

30. S's perception of discrimination in workforce   (1) no_ (2) yes
31. Couple's style of handling racism/discrim.
    1)   avoid (2) confront/discuss ____

32. Effect of racism/discrimination on marriage
    (0)   no (1) negative (2) positive ____

33. S's perception of African-American traditions followed in parents marriage   (1) no (2) yes
    (A)   first phase   _____
    (B)   second phase   _____
    (C)   third phase   _____

34. S's perception of role of African-American traditions in marital stability
    (0) no (1) negative (2) positive ____

35. Impact of S's family's reaction on decision to marry
    (0)   no (1) negative (2) positive ____

36. S's perception of race affecting economic factors
    (1)   no   (2) yes ____

Note: Items 1-24 were completed for all 120 respondents. Items 25 and beyond varied depending on the ethnic and racial characteristics of respondents.

Bibliography

Adams, B. (1979). Mate selection in the United States: A theoretical summarization. In W. R. Burr, R. Hill, F. I. Nye, & I. Reiss (Eds.), *Contemporary theories about the family*. New York: Free Press.

Aida, Y., & Falbo, T. (1991). Relationships between marital satisfaction, resources, and power strategies. *Sex Roles, 24*(1/2), 43–56.

Allen, A., & Thompson, T. (1984). Agreement, understanding, realization and feeling understood as predictors of communicative satisfaction in marital dyads. *Journal of Marriage and the Family* (November), 915–921.

Altrocchi, J., & Crosby, R. D. (1989). Clarifying and measuring the concept of traditional vs. egalitarian roles in marriages. *Sex Roles, 20*, 639–648.

Argyle, M., & Furnham, A. (1983). Sources of satisfaction and conflict in long-term relationships. *Journal of Marriage and the Family*, (August), 481–493.

Barnes, M. L., & Buss, D. M. (1985). Sex differences in the interpersonal behavior of married couples. *Journal of Personality and Social Psychology, 48*, 654–661.

Barry, W. A. (1970). Marriage research and conflict: An integrative review. *Psychological Bulletin, 73*, 41–54.

Bean, F. D., Curtis, R. L., & Marcum, J. P. (1977). Familism and marital satisfaction among Mexican Americans: The effect of family size, wife's labor force participation, and conjugal power. *Journal of Marriage and the Family, 39*, 759–767.

Belsky, J., Spanier, G. B., & Rivine, M. (1983). Stability and change in marriage across the transition to parenthood. *Journal of Marriage and the Family, 45*, 567–577.

Bem, S. L. (1987a). Gender schema theory and its implications for child development: Raising gender-aschematic children in a gender-schematic society. In M. R. Walsh (Ed.), *The psychology of women*. New Haven, Conn.: Yale University Press.

Bem, S. L. (1987b). Probing the promise of androgyny. In M. R. Walsh (Ed.), *The psychology of women*. New Haven, Conn.: Yale University Press.

Berg, J. H., & McQuinn, R. D. (1986). Attraction and exchange in continuing and noncontinuing dating relationships. *Journal of Personality and Social Psychology, 50* (5), 942–952.

Bernard, J. (1974). *The future of marriage*. New York: World.

Billings, A. (1979). Conflict resolution in distressed and nondistressed married couples. *Journal of Consulting and Clinical Psychology, 47*(2), 368–376.

Billingsley, A. (1990). Understanding African American family diversity. In J. Dewart (Ed.), *The state of black America 1990*. New York: National Urban League.

Birchler, G. R., & Webb, L. J. (1977). Discriminating interaction behaviors in happy and unhappy marriages. *Journal of Consulting and Clinical Psychology, 45*(3), 494–495.

Bjorksten, O., & Stewart, T. J. (1984). Contemporary trends in American marriages. In C. C. Nadelson & D.C. Polonsky (Eds.), *Marriage and divorce: A contemporary perspective*. New York: Guilford Press.

Blood, R. O. (1969). *Marriage*. (Second Edition). New York: The Free Press.

Blood, R. O., & Wolfe, D. M. (1960). *Husbands and wives: The dynamics of married living*. Glencoe, IL: The Free Press.

Bogdan, R., & Biklen, C. (1992). *Qualitative research for education: An introduction to theory and methods*. Boston: Allyn & Bacon.

Bowen, M. (1978). *Family therapy in clinical practice*. New York: Jason Aronson.

Broderick, J. E. (1981). A method for derivation of areas for assessment in marital relationships. *American Journal of Family Therapy, 9*, 25–34.

Broderick, J. E., & O'Leary, K. D. (1986). Contributions of affect, attitudes, and behavior to marital satisfaction. *Journal of Consulting and Clinical Psychology, 54*, 514–517.

Burgess, E., Wallin, P., & Schultz, G. (1954). *Courtship, engagement and marriage*. Philadelphia: J. P. Lippincott.

Buss, D. M. (1986). Human mate selection. *American Scientist, 73*(1), 47–51.

Cahn, D. D. (1983). Relative importance of perceived understanding in initial interaction and development of interpersonal relationships. *Psychological Reports, 52*, 923–929.

Calogeras, R. C. (1985). Early object-relations conflicts in marital interaction. *Psychoanalytic Review, 72* (1), 31–53.

Centers, R., Raven, B., & Rodrigues, A. (1971). Conjugal power structure: A re-examination. *American Sociological Review, 36*, 264–278.

Chapman, A. B. (1982). Male-female relations: How the past affects the present. In H. P. MacAdoo (Ed.), *Black families*, 2nd ed. Newbury Park, CA: Sage Publications.

Chelune, G. J., Rosenfeld, L. B., & Waring, E. M. (1985). Spouse disclosure patterns in distressed and nondistressed couples. *The American Journal of Family Therapy, 13* (4), 24–32.

Chodorow, N. (1978). *The reproduction of mothering: Psychoanalysis and the sociology of gender*. Berkeley: University of California Press.

Corrales, R. (1975). Power and satisfaction in early marriage. In R. E. Bromwell & D. H. Olsen (Eds.), *Power in families*. New York: John Wiley & Sons.

Cowan, C. P., Cowan, P. A., Heming, G., Garrett, E., Coysh, W. S., Curtis-Boles, H., & Boles, A. J., III (1985). Transitions to parenthood: His, hers, and theirs. *Journal of Family Issues, 6* (4), 451–481.

Cromwell, V. E., & Cromwell, R. E. (1978). Perceived dominance in decision-making and conflict resolution among Anglo, black, and Chicano couples. *Journal of Marriage and the Family, 40*, 749–759.

D'Agostino, J., & Day, S. (1991). Gender role orientation and preference for an intimate partner. *The Psychological Record, 41*, 321–328.

Demmett, C. C. (1992). *Marital satisfaction: A qualitative analysis*. Unpublished doctoral dissertation, Boston College.

Erikson, E. (1950). *Childhood and society*. New York: W. W. Norton.

Falicov, C. J. (1982). Mexican families. In M. McGoldrick, J. K. Pearce, and J. Giordant (Eds.), *Ethnicity and family therapy*. New York: Guilford Press.

Feingold, A. (1990). Gender differences in effects of physical attractiveness on romantic attraction: A comparison across five research paradigms. *Journal of Personality and Social Psychology, 59*, 981–993.

Feldman, S. S., & Nash, S. C. (1984). The transition from expectancy to parenthood: Impact of the firstborn child on men and women. *Sex Roles, 11*, 61–78.

Fowers, B. (1991). His and her marriages: A multivariate study of gender and marital satisfaction. *Sex Roles, 24*(3/4), 209–221.

Gilligan, C. (1982). *In a different voice: Psychological theory and women's development*. Cambridge, MA: Harvard University Press.

Gilligan, C. (1987). Women's place in man's life cycle. In C. Pinderhughes (Ed.), *Human behavior and the social environment*. Lexington, MA: Ginn Press.

Givens, P. B. (1978). Nonverbal basis of attraction. *Psychiatry, 41* (4), 346–359.

Goodwin, D., & Scanzoni, J. (1989). Couple consensus during marital joint decision-making: A context, process, outcome model. *Journal of Marriage and the Family, 51* (November), 943–956.

Gottman, J. M. (1982). Emotional responsiveness in marital conversation. *Journal of Communication, 32,* 108–120.

Gottman, J. M. (1991). Predicting the longitudinal course of marriages. *Journal of Marital and Family Therapy, 17,* 3–7.

Gottman, J. M., & Krokoff, L. J. (1989). Marital interaction and satisfaction: A longitudinal view. *Journal of Consulting and Clinical Psychology, 57* (1), 47–52.

Gottman, J. M., & Porterfield, A. L. (1981). Communicative competence in the nonverbal behavior of married couples. *Journal of Marriage and the Family, 4,* 817–824.

Gray-Little, B. (1982). Marital quality and power processes among black couples. *Journal of Marriage and the Family, 44,* 633–646.

Gray-Little, B., & Burks, N. (1983). Power and satisfaction in marriage: A review and critique. *Psychological Bulletin, 93*(3), 513–538.

Grover, K. J., Russell, C. S., Schumm, W. R., & Paff-Bergen, L. A. (1985). Mate selection processes and marital satisfaction. *Family Relations, 34,* 383–386.

Haefner, P., Notorius, C., & Pellegrini, D. (1991). Determinants of satisfaction with marital discussions: An exploration of husband-wife differences. *Behavioral Assessment, 13,* 67–82.

Hamel, C. (1993). Marital stability: A qualitative psychological study of African American couples. Unpublished doctoral dissertation, Boston College.

Hicks, M. W., & Platt, M. (1970). Marital happiness and stability: A review of the research in the sixties. *Journal of Marriage and the Family, 32,* 553–574.

Hiller, D. V., & Philliber, W. W. (1986). The division of labor in contemporary marriage: Expectations, perceptions, and performance. *Social Problems, 33*(3), 191–201.

Hines, P. M., & Boyd-Franklin, N. (1982). Black families. In M. McGoldrick, J. K. Pearce, & J. Giordano (Eds.), *Ethnicity and family therapy.* New York: Guilford Press.

Holahan, C. K. (1984). Marital attitudes over 40 years: A longitudinal and cohort analysis. *Journal of Gerontology, 39,* 49–57.

Holtzman, E. H., & Gilbert, L. A. (1987). Social support networks for parenting and psychological well being among dual-career Mexican American families. *Journal of Community Psychology, 15,* 176–185.

Honeycutt, J. M. (1986). A model of marital functioning based on an attraction paradigm and social-penetration dimensions. *Journal of Marriage and the Family, 48,* 651–667.

Hyde, J. S., & Phillis, D. E. (1979). Androgny across the life span. *Developmental Psychology, 15*(3), 334–336.

Jackson, B., & Hardiman, R. (1983). Racial identity development: Implications for managing the multiracial workforce. *The NTL Manager's Handbook.* NTL Institute, 107–113.

Johnson, S., & Greenberg, L. (1987). Emotionally focused marital therapy: An overview. *Psychotherapy, 24* (38), 552–660.

Jourard, S. M. (1971). *Self-disclosure: An experimental analysis of the transparent self.* New York: Wiley-Interscience.

Kahn, A., & McGaughy, T. (1977). Distance and closeness: When moving close produces increased likeness. *Sociometry, 40* (2), 138–144.

Kahn, M. (1979). Nonverbal communication and marital satisfaction. *Family Process, 9,* 449–456.

Kanter, L. (1993). Marital stability: A qualitative psychological study of Jewish couples. Unpublished doctoral dissertation, Boston College.

Kayser, K. (1993). *When love dies: The process of marital disaffection.* New York: Guilford Press.

Kayser, K., & Himle, D. (1991). *Marital intimacy: A model for clinical assessment and intervention.* New York: The Haworth Press.

Keefe, S. E. (1984). Acculturation and the extended family among urban Mexican Americans. In A.M. Padilla (Ed.), *Acculturation: Theory models, and some new findings.* Boulder, CO: Westview Press.

Kelley, D., & Burgoon, J. (1991). Understanding marital satisfaction and couple type as functions of relational expectations. *Human Communication Research, 18*(1), 40–69.

Kelly, E. L., & Conley, J. (1987). Personality and compatibility: A prospective analysis of marital stability and marital satisfaction. *Journal of Personality and Social Psychology, 52* (1), 27–40.

Kingsbury, N., & Scanzoni, J. (1989). Process, power and decision outcomes among dual-career couples. *Journal of Comparative Family Studies, XX* (2), 231–246.

Komarovsky, M. (1962). *Blue-Collar marriage.* New York: Vintage Books.

Komarovsky, M. (1973). Cultural contradictions and sex roles: the masculine case. *American Journal of Sociology, 78,* 873–884.

Koski, K. J., & Steinberg, L. (1990). Parenting satisfaction of mothers during midlife. *Journal of Youth and Adolescence, 19* (5), 25–38.

Kvale, S. (1983). The qualitative research interview: A phenomenological and hermeneutical mode of understanding. *Journal of Phenomenological Psychology, 14,* 171–196.

Lauer, R. H., Lauer, J. C., & Kerr, S. T. (1990). The long-term marriage: Perceptions of stability and satisfaction. *International Journal of Aging and Human Development, 31,* 189–195.

Levenson, R., Carstensen, L., & Gottman, J. (1993). Long-term marriage: Age, gender and satisfaction. *Psychology and Aging, 8* (3), 301–313.

Levinson, D. (1986). A concept of adult development. *American Psychologist, 41* (1), 3–13.

Lewis, J. M. (1988a). The transition to parenthood: II. Stability and change in marital structure. *Family Process, 27,* 273–283.

Lewis, J. M. (1988b). The transition to parenthood: I. The rating of prenatal marital competence. *Family Process, 27,* 149–165.

Lewis, R. A., & Spanier, G. B. (1979). Theorizing about the quality and stability of marriage. In W. R. Burr, R. Hill, F. I. Nye & I. L. Reiss (Eds.), *Contemporary theories about the family.* Glencoe, IL: The Free Press.

Lombardo, J., Francis, P., & Brown, S. (1988). Sex role and opposite sex interpersonal attraction. *Perceptual and Motor Skills, 67,* 855–869.

MacAdoo, H. P. (Ed.). (1988). *Black families* (2nd Ed.). Newbury Park, CA: Sage.

Mack, D. (1978). The power relationship in black families and white families. In R. Staples (Ed.), *The black American reference book.* Englewood Cliffs, NJ: Prentice-Hall.

Margolin, L., & White, L. (1987). The continuing role of physical attractiveness in marriage. *Journal of Marriage and the Family, 49,* 21–27.

Markman, H. (1981). Prediction of marital distress: A 5-year follow-up. *Journal of Consulting and Clinical Psychology, 49* (5), 760–762.

Mason, K. O., & Bumpass, L. L. (1975). U.S. women's sex role ideology, 1970. *American Journal of Sociology, 80,* 1212–1219.

Masterson, J. (1985). *The real self: A developmental self and objects relations approach.* New York: Brunner/Mazel.

Mathes, E. W., & Moore, C. L. (1985). Reik's complementarity theory of romantic love. *The Journal of Social Psychology, 125* (3), 321–327.

McGee, J., & Wells, K. (1982). Gender typing and androgyny in later life. *Human Development, 25,* 116–139.

Mengden, S. (1994). Marital stability: A qualitative psychological study of Mexican American couples. Unpublished doctoral dissertation, Boston College.

Middleton, R., & Putney, S. (1960). Dominance in decisions in the family: Race and class differences. In C. V. Willie (Ed.), The family life of black people. Columbus, OH: Charles E. Merrill.

Miller, B. C., & Sollie, D. L. (1980). Normal stresses during the transition to parenthood. *Family Relations, 29,* 459–465.

Miller, J. B. (1986). *Toward a new psychology of women.* Boston: Beacon Press.

Miller, J. B. (1988). Connections, disconnections and violations. *Work in Progress.* Wellesley, MA: Stone Center Working Paper Series.

Moon, S., Dillon, D., & Sprenkle, D. (1990). Family therapy and qualitative research. *Journal of Marital and Family Therapy, 16*(4), 357–373.

Moore, M., & Butler, D. (1989). Predictive aspects of nonverbal courtship in women. *Semiotica, 76* (3–4), 205–212.

Murillo, N. (1971). The Mexican American family. In N. N. Wagner & M. J. Haug (Eds.), *Chicanos: Social and psychological perspectives*. St. Louis: C. V. Mosby Co.

Nadelson, C. C., Polonsky, D. C., & Matthews, M. A. (1984). Marriage as a developmental process. In C. C. Nadelson & D. C. Polonsky (Eds.), *Marriage and divorce*. New York: Guilford Press.

Nichols, W. C. (1978, April). The marriage relationship. *The Family Coordinator*, 185–191.

Noller, P. (1984). *Nonverbal communication and marital interaction*. Oxford, England: Pergamon Press.

Offer, D., & Schonert-Reichl, K. L. (1992). Debunking the myths of adolescence: Findings from recent research. *Journal of the American Academy of Child and Adolescent Psychiatry, 31*, 1003–1014.

O'Neil, J. M., Fishman, D. M., & Kinsella-Shaw, M. (1987). Dual-career couples' career transitions and normative dilemmas: A preliminary assessment model. *The Counseling Psychologist, 15* (s), 50–96.

Orlofsky, J. (1982). Psychological androgyny, sex typing and sex role ideology as predictors of male-female initial attraction. *Sex Roles, 8*(10).

Parks, M., Stan, C., & Eggert, L. (1983). Romantic involvement and social network involvement. *Social Psychology Quarterly, 46* (2), 116–131.

Pinderhughes, E. (1982). Afro American families and the victim system. In M. McGoldrick, J. K. Pearce, & J. Giordano (Eds.), *Ethnicity and family therapy*. New York: Guilford Press.

Pinderhughes, E. (1989). *Understanding race, ethnicity, and power: Key to efficacy in clinical practice*. New York: Free Press.

Podbelski, J. J. (1993). Factors involved in marital stability. Unpublished doctoral dissertation, Boston College.

Prochaska, J., & Prochaska, J. (1978). Twentieth century trends in marriage and marital therapy. In T. Paolino and B. McCrady (Eds.), *Marriage and marital therapy*. New York: Brunner/Mazel.

Reibstein, J. (1988). Family therapy and sex role development throughout the life-cycle: A useful concept. *Journal of Family Therapy, 10*, 153–166.

Roberts, W. L. (1979). Significant elements in the relationship of long-married couples. *International Journal of Aging and Human Development, 10* (3), 265–272.

Robertson, I. (1987). *Sociology*. New York: Worth Publishers.

Rollins, B. C., & Cannon, K. L. (1974). Marital satisfaction over the family life cycle: A reevaluation. *Journal of Marriage and the Family, 36*, 271–282.

Rollins, B. C., & Feldman, H. (1970). Marital satisfaction over the family life cycle. *Journal of Marriage and the Family, 32*, 20–27.

Rosenbaum, M. E. (1986). Comment on a proposed two-stage theory of relationship formation: First, repulsion; then, attraction. *Journal of Personality and Social Psychology, 51* (6), 1171–1172.

Rosenfeld, L. B., & Welsh, S. M. (1985). Differences in self-disclosure in dual-career and single-career marriages. *Communication Monographs, 52*, 253–263.

Rubin, L. B. (1983). *Intimate strangers.* New York: Harper & Row.

Rubin, L. B. (1976). *Worlds of pain.* New York: Basic Books.

Scanzoni, J. (1968). A social system analysis of dissolved and existing marriages. *Journal of Marriage and the Family, 30*, 452–461.

Scanzoni, J., & Szinovaca, M. (1980). *Family decision-making.* Beverly Hills: Sage Publications.

Scarf, M. (1986, November). Intimate partners. *Atlantic Monthly, 11*, 45–93.

Schaefer, M., & Olson, D. (1981). Assessing intimacy: The PAIR Inventory. *Journal of Marital and Family Therapy*, 47–59.

Schafer, R. B., & Keith, P. M. (1981). Equity in marital roles across the family life cycle. *Journal of Marriage and the Family, 43*, 359–367.

Schoen, R., Woolredge, J., & Thomas, B. (1989). Ethnic and educational effects on marriage choice. *Social Science Quarterly, 79* (3), 617–629.

Shachar, R. (1991). His and her marital satisfaction: The double standard. *Sex Roles, 25* (7/8), 451–467.

Silverberg, S. B., & Steinberg, L. (1987). Adolescent autonomy, parent-adolescent conflict and parental well-being. *Journal of Youth and Adolescence, 16* (3), 293–312.

Simpson, J., Lerma, M., & Gangstead, S. W. (1990). Perception of physical attractiveness: Mechanisms involved in the maintenance of romantic relationships. *Journal of Personality and Social Psychology, 59* (6), 1192–1201.

Simpson, J. A., & Gangstead, S. W. (1992). Sociosexuality and romantic partner choice. *Journal of Personality, 60* (1), 31–49.

Sitton, S., & Rippee, E. (1986). Women still want marriage: Sex differences in lonely hearts advertisements. *Psychological Reports, 58* (1), 257–258.

Sluzki, C., & Beavin, J. (1977). Symmetry and complementarity: An operational definition and a typology of dyads. In P. Watzlawick & J. Weaklard (Eds.), *The interactional view.* New York: W. W. Norton Co.

Spanier, G. B., & Fleer, B. (1980). Factors sustaining marriage: Factors in adjusting to divorce. In *Families Today*, U.S. Department of Health, Education & Welfare, Science Monographs, 205–231.

Spanier, G. B., & Lewis, R. A. (1980). Marital quality: A review of the seventies. *Journal of Marriage and the Family*, 825–839.

Spanier, G. B., Lewis, R. A., & Cole, C. L. (1975). Marital adjustment over the family life cycle: The issue of curvilinearity. *Journal of Marriage and the Family, 37*, (May) 263–275.

Sprecher, S. (1989). The importance to males and females of physical attractiveness, earning potential, and expressiveness in initial attraction. *Sex Roles, 21* (9/10), 591–607.

Sprenkle, D. H., & Olson, D. H. (1978). Circumplex model of marital systems: An empirical study of clinic and nonclinic couples. *Journal of Marriage and Family Counseling, 4*, 59–74.

Staples, R. (1988). An overview of race and marital status. In H. P. McAdoo (Ed.), *Black families,* 2nd. Ed. Newbury Park, CA: Sage Publications.

Steinberg, L. (1981). Family processes at adolescence: A developmental perspective. *Family Therapy, 14* (2), 77–85.

Storaasli, R. D., & Markman, H. J. (1990). Relationship problems in the early stages of marriage: A longitudinal investigation. *Journal of Family Psychology, 4* (1), 80–98.

Strauss, A., & Corbin, J. (1990). *Basics of qualitative research: Grounded theory procedures and techniques.* Newbury Park, CA: Sage.

Surra, C. A. (1990). Research and theory on mate selection and premarital relationships in the 1980's. *Journal of Marriage and the Family, 52*, 844.

Surrey, J. L. (1984). The "self-in-relation": A theory of women's development. *Work in Progress, No. 13.* Wellesley, MA: Stone Center Working Papers Series.

TenHouten, W. (1970). The black family: Myth and reality. *Psychiatry, 2*, 145–153.

Thompson, L., & Walker, A. (1989). Gender in families: Women and men in marriage, work and parenthood. *Journal of Marriage and the Family, 51*, 845–871.

Vaillant, C. O., & Vaillant, G. E. (1993). Is the U-curve of marital satisfaction an illusion? A 40-year study of marriage. *Journal of Marriage and the Family, 55*, 230–239.

Vannoy, D. (1991). Social differentiation, contemporary marriage and human development, *Journal of Family Issues, 12* (3), 251–267.

Vega, W. A. (1990). Hispanic families in the 1980's: A decade of research. *Journal of Marriage and the Family, 52*, 1015–1024.

Watzlawick, P., Beavin, J., & Jackson, D. (1967). *Pragmatics of human communication: study of interactional patterns, pathologies and parodoxes.* New York: W. W. Norton & Co.

White, K., Speisman, J., Jackson, D., Bartis, S., and Costos, D. (1986). Intimacy, maturity and its correlation in young married couples. *Journal of Personality and Social Psychology, 50*, 152–162.

White, L. K. (1990). Determinants of divorce: A review of research in the eighties. *Journal of Marriage and the Family, 52*, 904–912.

Williams, N. (1990). *The Mexican American family: Tradition and change.* Dix Hills, NY: General Hall.

Willie, C. V. (1985). *Black and white families: A study in complimentarity.* Bayside, NY: General Hall.

Willie, C. V. (1976). *A new look at black families.* Bayside, NY: General Hall.

Willie, C. V., & Greenblatt, S. L. (1978). Four classic studies of power relationships in black families. *Journal of Marriage and the Family, 40,* 691–696.

Winnicott, D. W. (1965). *The maturational process and the facilitating environment.* New York: International Universities Press.

Ybarra, L. (1978). Marital decision-making and the role of machismo in the Chicano family. *DeColores Journal, 6,* 32–47.

Youniss, J., & Ketterlinus, R. D. (1987). Communication and connectedness in mother and father adolescent relationships. *Journal of Youth and Adolescence, 16* (3), 265–280.

Zube, M. (1982). Changing behavior and outlook of aging men and women: Implications for marriage in the middle and later years. *Family Relations, 31,* 147–156.

Index

About the Authors

RICHARD A. MACKEY is Professor, Graduate School of Social Work, Boston College.

BERNARD A. O'BRIEN is Associate Professor, Department of Counseling, Developmental Psychology, and Research Methods, Boston College.

Among their earlier publications are *Ego Psychology and Clinical Practice* and articles in *Journal of Teaching in Social Work* and *Social Work with Groups*. The authors have extensive experience in the practice of marital therapy.